Vertical Heartland

A Rock Climber's Guide To
Southern Illinois

by
Eric Ulner

Photography by David Hart

Published by Second West

ISBN 0-9648053-0-8

Road maps have been redrawn from county road maps provided by the Illinois Department of Transportation.

Every wall of the cliffs was surveyed with a compass for the hand drawn overview maps to provide more accurate detail than USGS topo maps.

Front cover photo: Kathy Ulner on the second pitch of *The Blue Roof,* 5.10, Draper's Bluff.

Back cover photo: Spring time at Jackson Falls north water fall.

Published and Distributed by Second West
PO Box 3873 Carbondale, IL 62902
618-549-1189

Climbing Guidebooks Covering Southern Illinois

The Gritstone Mountaineer, by Adam Grosowsky, 1976
50 Short Climbs in the Midwest, by Alan Baggs, 1978
A Climber's Guide to the Mid South, by Jim Detterline, 1981
Shades of Gray, by Jim Detterline, 1981 (ice climbing guide)
S.I.C. Routes, by Jim Thurmond, 1991
Jackson Falls, by Michael Simpson, 1989, 1990, 1995
Vertical Heartland, by Eric Ulner, 1993, 1994, 2nd Edition- 1996

Warning!

Climbing is a potentially dangerous activity. This book is not a substitute for instruction. The user/reader of this book assumes full liability for his/her actions that result in injury or death. The author, publisher, and distributors are held blameless in any event resulting in injury or death. Do yourself and emergency medical services a big favor- If in doubt, seek qualified instruction.

INTRODUCTION

Welcome to Round 2. Why a second edition? Much has happened since the two prints of the first edition were published. There have been changes in land ownership and management policies, area improvements, and new climbing routes- all worthy impetus. Dave & I figured we'd keep up with happenings & demand. We hope you enjoy the improvements.

-Eric Ulner

THANKS!

My wife Kathy- for everything.
Sean and Tim Scuras- for getting me started with rock climbing in the first place.
My parents- for letting me go with Sean & Tim, even though we were all just punks.
My climbing partners through the years- for motivation & all those great catches.
Debra Eddison- for time, expertise, & writing contribution on area habitat.
Dr. Arnold Ulner & Gary Hart- for editing support.
Dr. Robert Haugh- for trust & good times.
John Payne- for diligence in leading the Southern Illinois Climbers' Alliance, especially as our representative in the Illinois Dept. of Natural Resources Conservation Caucus.
The Access Fund- You might not be doing much climbing here if it weren't for them. Support them by becoming a member!
The American Mountain Guides Association- for existing & education.
The Shawnee National Forest Management- for accepting rock climbing into their Revised Management Plan.
The Illinois Dept. of Natural Resources- for giving the Southern Illinois Climbers' Alliance a seat in their Conservation Congress.
Beth Shimp (Forest Service) & Todd Fink (Illinois DNR)- for writing contributions. See dedication to Todd, page 23.
Jim Myers, Jay Bruce, & Tim Nation- for expertise & technical support.
Jeff Armit, Climatologist- for weather history.
Dr. Steve Sims- for motivation and guidance.
Alan Carrier- for superb craftsmanship in creating the signboard for Jackson Falls.
Buddy Guy and Blues Traveler- for coming to Carbondale during the spring of '92- a remarkable turn of events in meeting David Hart in the ticket line at 3:00 a.m.
SounDesign Co.- for manufacturing the alarm clock that awakened me to go buy tickets.
Jackson, our dog- for providing scale in some of the cliff photos.

TABLE OF CONTENTS

What has the Southern Illinois Climbers' Alliance been doing for you lately?...

- SICA gained the acceptance of rock climbing into the Revised Management Plan of the Shawnee National Forest. Rock climbers are now an official user group of the forest.

- SICA obtained a membership seat in the Illinois Department of Natural Resources' (IDNR) Conservation Congress. A SICA representative regularly attends meetings.

- SICA played a definitive role in the IDNR's assurance that rock climbing will be grandfathered in at Cedar and Draper's Bluffs. Meaning- without SICA, no Cedar and Draper's Bluffs.

- SICA and the Access Fund cost-shared with the Shawnee National Forest for the Jackson Falls parking area upgrade.

Since 1991, Southern Illinois Climber's Alliance (SICA) has been successfully working to keep rock climbing a viable activity in Southern Illinois for climbers from around the world.

Southern Illinois Climbers' Alliance
P.O. Box 3873
Carbondale, IL 62902-3873

...We've been persistent.

5

the ACCESS FUND

Access: It's Everybody's Concern

The Access Fund, a national, non-profit climbers organization, is working to keep you climbing. The Access Fund helps preserve access and protect the environment by providing funds for land acquisitions and climber-support facilities, financing scientific studies, publishing educational materials, promoting low-impact climbing, and providing start-up money, legal counsel and other resources to local climbers' coalitions.

Climbers can help preserve access **by being responsible users of climbing areas. Here are some practical ways to support climbing:**

- **Commit yourself to "leaving no trace."**
  Pick up litter around campgrounds and the crags. Let your actions inspire others.

- **Dispose of human waste properly.**
  Use toilets whenever possible. If none are available, choose a spot at least 50 meters from any water source.
  Dig a hole 6" (15 cm) deep, then bury your waste afterwards.
  Always pack out toilet paper (use zip-lock plastic bags).

- **Use existing trails.**
  Avoid cutting switchbacks and trampling vegetation.

- **Use discretion when placing bolts and other "fixed" protection.**
  Camouflage all anchors with rock-colored paint.
  Use chains for rappel stations, or leave rock-colored webbing.

- **Respect restrictions which protect natural resources and cultural artifacts.**
  Appropriate restrictions can include prohibitions of climbing around Indian rock art, pioneer inscriptions, and on certain formations during raptor nesting season.
  Power drills are illegal in wilderness areas.
  Never chisel or otherwise manufacture holds in natural rock-- no other practice so seriously threatens our sport.

- **Park in designated areas.**
  Try not to park not in undeveloped, vegetated areas.
  Carpool to the crags!

- **Maintain a low profile.**
  Other people have the same right to undisturbed enjoyment of natural areas as you do.

- **Respect private property.**
  Don't trespass in order to climb.

- **Join or form a group to deal with access issues in your area.**
  Consider clean-ups, trail building or maintenance, and other "goodwill" projects.

- **Join the Access Fund.**
  To become a member, *simply make a tax-deductible donation of any amount.* Only by working together can we preserve both access and our natural resources.

The Access Fund.
Preserving America's diverse climbing resources.

The Access Fund • PO Box 17010 • Boulder, CO 80308

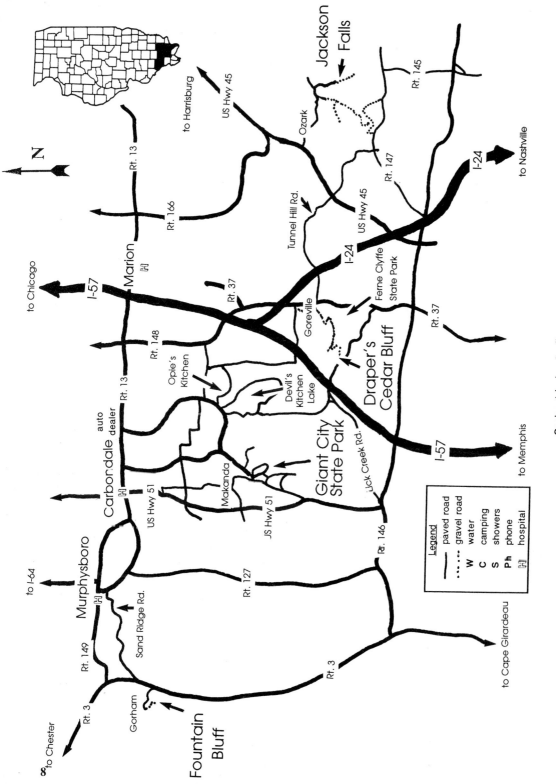

N

to Chicago
I-57
Marion Ⓗ
Rt. 13
Rt. 166
to Harrisburg
US Hwy 45
Ozark
Rt. 145
Jackson Falls
Rt. 147
Rt. 37
I-24
US Hwy 45
Tunnel Hill Rd.
I-24
to Nashville
Ferne Clyffe State Park
Goreville
Draper's Cedar Bluff
Rt. 37
Rt. 148
Opie's Kitchen
Rt. 13
Carbondale Ⓗ
auto dealer
Devil's Kitchen Lake
Giant City State Park
Lick Creek Rd.
I-57
to Memphis
US Hwy 51
Makanda
US Hwy 51
Murphysboro Ⓗ
Rt. 149
to I-64
Sand Ridge Rd.
Rt. 127
Rt. 146
Rt. 3
to Cape Girardeau
Gorham
Rt. 3
Fountain Bluff
to Chester

Legend
—— paved road
••••• gravel road
W   water
C   camping
S   showers
Ph phone
Ⓗ   hospital

Scale: 1 inch = 6 miles

8

"FOSTERING PROFESSIONALISM AND REPRESENTING AMERICAN MOUNTAIN GUIDES WHILE PROVIDING A FORUM FOR THE EXCHANGE OF IDEAS INCLUDING EDUCATION AND TRAINING, AND SERVING THE PUBLIC INTEREST BY ADVOCATING RESPONSIBLE LAND USE, ACCESS AND CLIMBER SAFETY."

AMERICAN MOUNTAIN GUIDES ASSOCIATION
710 10TH STREET, SUITE 101
GOLDEN, CO 80401
303-271-0984

Local Climbing Time Line

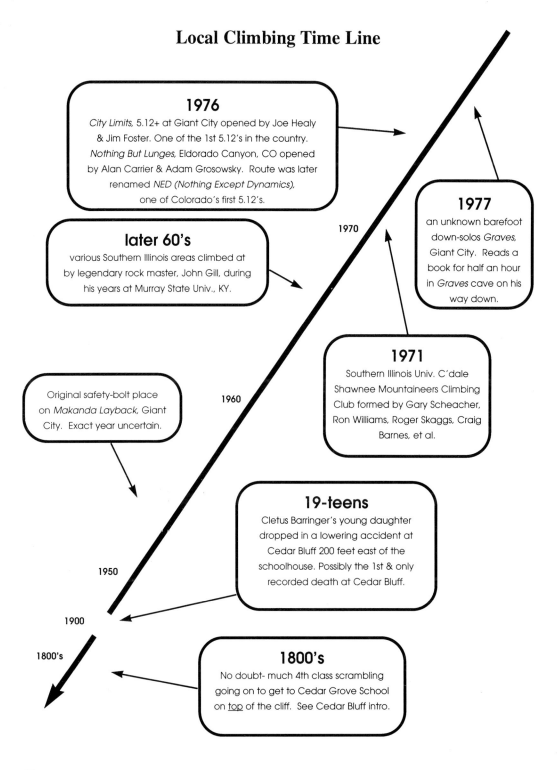

1976
City Limits, 5.12+ at Giant City opened by Joe Healy & Jim Foster. One of the 1st 5.12's in the country. *Nothing But Lunges,* Eldorado Canyon, CO opened by Alan Carrier & Adam Grosowsky. Route was later renamed *NED (Nothing Except Dynamics),* one of Colorado's first 5.12's.

1977
an unknown barefoot down-solos *Graves,* Giant City. Reads a book for half an hour in *Graves* cave on his way down.

later 60's
various Southern Illinois areas climbed at by legendary rock master, John Gill, during his years at Murray State Univ., KY.

1971
Southern Illinois Univ. C'dale Shawnee Mountaineers Climbing Club formed by Gary Scheacher, Ron Williams, Roger Skaggs, Craig Barnes, et al.

Original safety-bolt place on *Makanda Layback,* Giant City. Exact year uncertain.

19-teens
Cletus Barringer's young daughter dropped in a lowering accident at Cedar Bluff 200 feet east of the schoolhouse. Possibly the 1st & only recorded death at Cedar Bluff.

1800's
No doubt- much 4th class scrambling going on to get to Cedar Grove School on <u>top</u> of the cliff. See Cedar Bluff intro.

1970

1960

1950

1900

1800's

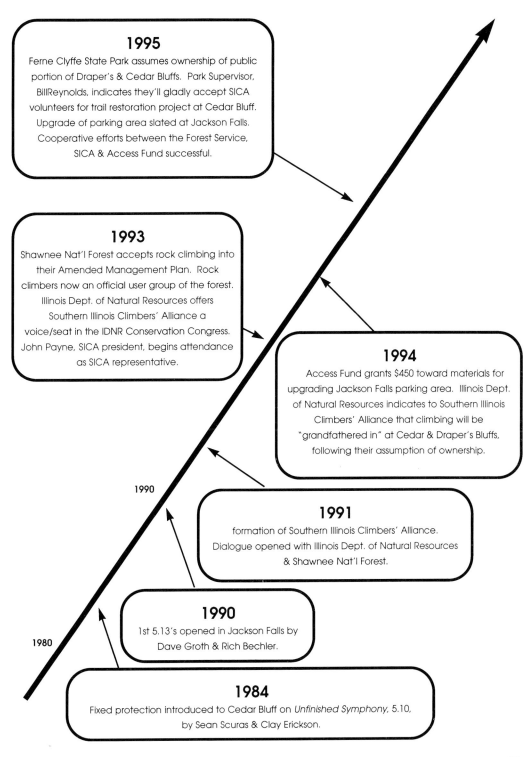

1995

Ferne Clyffe State Park assumes ownership of public portion of Draper's & Cedar Bluffs. Park Supervisor, BillReynolds, indicates they'll gladly accept SICA volunteers for trail restoration project at Cedar Bluff. Upgrade of parking area slated at Jackson Falls. Cooperative efforts between the Forest Service, SICA & Access Fund successful.

1993

Shawnee Nat'l Forest accepts rock climbing into their Amended Management Plan. Rock climbers now an official user group of the forest. Illinois Dept. of Natural Resources offers Southern Illinois Climbers' Alliance a voice/seat in the IDNR Conservation Congress. John Payne, SICA president, begins attendance as SICA representative.

1994

Access Fund grants $450 toward materials for upgrading Jackson Falls parking area. Illinois Dept. of Natural Resources indicates to Southern Illinois Climbers' Alliance that climbing will be "grandfathered in" at Cedar & Draper's Bluffs, following their assumption of ownership.

1990

1991

formation of Southern Illinois Climbers' Alliance. Dialogue opened with Illinois Dept. of Natural Resources & Shawnee Nat'l Forest.

1990

1st 5.13's opened in Jackson Falls by Dave Groth & Rich Bechler.

1980

1984

Fixed protection introduced to Cedar Bluff on *Unfinished Symphony*, 5.10, by Sean Scuras & Clay Erickson.

THE "NATURE" OF SOUTHERN ILLINOIS
by Debra Eddison

HISTORY OF THE SHAWNEE NATIONAL FOREST

Envision the Shawnee National Forest at the turn of the century. Are you picturing towering trees, lush vegetation, the forests teeming with wildlife? Well if you are, you've definitely got the wrong picture, or for that matter, the wrong place. The truth is, the Shawnee National Forest as we know it today, was basically non-existent in the 1800's. The first settlers that came to Southern Illinois believed strongly in the ideal of divide and conquer. Additionally, 99 percent of the first settlers in Southern Illinois were farmers. Now can you guess what the land looked like back in the "good old days"? Almost all of the beautiful land we are so familiar with today was reduced to agricultural fields, or cleared completely for commercial timber harvest. Erosion was eating away at the face of the land, while land use management was virtually unheard of.

In 1933, Teddy Roosevelt created the CCC (Civilian Conservation Corps). The Civilian Conservation Corps was created partially in response to high unemployment rates after World War I, and to the fact that most farmers had lost their lands. The objective was to create jobs for people while making work related to Natural Resources. The CCC, along with other Forest Service employees, were essentially responsible for creating the Shawnee National Forest as we know it today. Since the 1930's, they had forested at least 40,000 acres of land. The CCC was also responsible for making many of the trails, roads, campsites and buildings in the area, many of which still exist. A good example of a CCC constructed building is the Lodge at Giant City State Park. Let's have a warm round of applause for the CCC, ladies and gentlemen, for they have created your forest.

FOREST TYPES OF ILLINOIS

When thinking of Illinois terrain, farm land is a common first thought. Although a fairly accurate one, let's not forget that 12% of the state is forested. The Shawnee National Forest, a very special ecosystem, accounts for much of that 12% of forest land. In general, the forests of Southern Illinois are un-evenly aged, with the majority of them being older than 60 years. Southern counties have the greatest variety of tree species. Jackson County checks in with 145 species, Pope with 129, and Union with 128. There are several different forest types occurring in Southern Illinois.

Oak/Hickory- The Oak/Hickory forest is the major forest type found in Illinois. There have been 22 species of Oak, and 16 species of Hickory found in the state. These forests support an abundance of wildlife while yielding large quantities of foods including acorn and hickory nuts. Recent trends show that Oak/Hickory forests have decreased by 14%.

Maple/Beech- Maple/Beech is another forest type commonly found in Southern Illinois. This forest is quickly becoming more successful than the Oak/Hickory forest because of the Maple's ability to tolerate shade. Shade tolerance allows it to reproduce successfully under closed canopies, or low light conditions. In the past 25 years, Maples have increased from 0.025 to 1.046 million acres!

Elm, Ash, Soft Maple- Bottomland forests contain these tree types, comprising one-third of Illinois forests. They are low lying and wet. Water may cover all or just part of the land during certain times of the year.

Oak-Gum/Cypress- Another type of forest found in Southern Illinois is the Oak-Gum/Cypress forest. It is mostly found in the bottom lands of Southern Illinois. It's distribution used to be wide spread, but due to the very large nature of the cypress tree, most cypress forests were cut for timber. Cypress trees can grow over

100 feet tall and over 8 feet in diameter. They are definitely worth seeing. The Cypress swamp of the Cache River is a local favorite.

WILDLIFE OF THE AREA

Southern Illinois contains many diverse ecosystems, each hosting a wide variety of wildlife. Opportunities for wildlife observation are plentiful. But allow me to first explain "wildlife observation". It is a detailed concentration of many senses, including seeing, hearing and sometimes smelling. You may get to know some animals on an "up close and personal" basis. Other animals may be more elusive, giving you the chance to only hear them without even a glimpse. So, keep all senses open to enhance your wildlife observation. Now that you are ready, I will continue with some brief facts concerning some of the animals of Southern Illinois. The change of day and night sets the scene for creatures. Therefore, animals that are most frequently active at night, dusk, or dawn, will be distinguished with an asterisk (*).

1. MAMMALS: There are approximately sixty-seven species of mammals found in the state of Illinois. Ten species are currently on the threatened and endangered list, while nine species have been extirpated (no longer found).

Flying Squirrels- Smallest of the tree squirrels. The flying squirrels are the only nocturnal and carnivorous species of squirrel. It feeds on nuts, berries, small insects and sometimes vertebrate flesh. It does not truly fly, but uses the folds of skin stretched between it's forelegs and hindlegs to glide. Its call is faint and bird-like.

Grey and Fox Squirrels- Both species occur in the Southern Illinois area. The distinguishing factor between the two is the color (the Fox Squirrel is red). These squirrels are active in the day time. They may be seen collecting and storing nuts for the long winter months. They locate their buried nuts in the winter by sense of smell.

Chipmunk- This critter may be seen on the ground or in trees collecting acorns. Its life is that of never ending food gathering and storage. Major predators of this animal are the weasel, fox, hawk, and bobcat.

Long-tailed Weasel- One of the most ferocious hunters, weasels are wholly carnivorous. Their diet consists mostly of mice, but they will also take rabbits, shrews, rats, and birds, including poultry. They are known to attack prey several times their size. Weasels den in the ground, sometimes in abandoned burrows. They used to be prized by trappers, but today their pelts are not of great value.

White-footed Mouse, Deer Mouse- Both very common in Southern Illinois. They're active year-round, providing great prey for owls, fox, coyotes, & anything else that can get their paws/teeth on them.

Beavers and Muskrats*- These very large rodents can be found about riverbanks, streams, lakes and ponds. Both are primarily nocturnal and excellent swimmers. Both species have suffered pressures of unregulated trapping. The beaver had actually disappeared from much of it's original range, but has been reintroduced over most of the continent (including Illinois).

River Otters- Once highly endangered, the Illinois has begun efforts to recover/reintroduce River Otters. Their habitat is primarily along rivers, lakes, and ponds along wooded areas. If you see one of these creatures frolicking about, please call the Illinois Department of Natural Resources at (217) 782-6384. They monitor the success of this project. Note details such as location and size.

Skunks*- Mostly nocturnal, but active in the day as well. If you run across one of these critters, do your best not to frighten it. If you or your dog are sprayed, seek immediate immersion in a bath of tomato juice. Fluid spray from a skunk is said to cause intense pain to the eyes and fleeting loss of vision. Especially be aware of the extremely protective mother skunk with her young.

Raccoon*- One of the many possible visitors at your campsite, the raccoon is wide spread throughout Illinois. They are almost always seen alone at night along streamsides collecting crayfish, frogs, worms, and fish.

Opossum*- These slow moving creatures are nocturnal and solitary. In a frightened state, an opossum will sometimes freeze or play dead. They have a varied diet including insects, snakes, frogs, mammals and fruits. These critters can most often be seen on the side of the road dining on roadkill (or flattened in the road- E.U.).

Rabbits*- Very common in Southern Illinois. The old saying holds true, as this animal breeds from February through September. However this animal's birth rate is almost near to it's death rate, as few rabbits live more than one year. They are active all year-round and therefore provide an excellent food source for many species.

Devil's Walking Stick

Fox*- These animals are fairly common to the Southern Illinois area. Although, they may be difficult to observe because of their elusive manner. Their diet is varied with season. They feed mostly on cherries, apples, corn, berries, grapes, acorns, grasses, and a large amount of insects in the summer. In the winter, they will eat birds and mammals such as mice, rabbits, squirrels and woodchucks. Although mostly nocturnal, they may be seen on dark cloudy days.

Coyote*- Very common in most parts of the country, this animal has adapted very well to human activity. Mostly nocturnal, your chances of hearing this animal are far better than seeing one. Distinct vocalizations include a series of barks and yelps, followed by a prolonged howl, and ending with short and sharp yaps. Coyotes, unlike fox, hunt in smaller groups or pairs. These vocalizations keep the group alert to locations of its members, and reunites them when separated.

Bobcat*- Once plentiful in Southern Illinois, habitat destruction and unregulated trapping have decreased the population dramatically. A sighting of this animal is very rare. If anything, you may hear its piercing scream without ever seeing it. If you are lucky enough to sight a bobcat, contact the Cooperative Wildlife Research Lab at Southern Illinois University at, 618-536-7766. The University is conducting a study to determine the status, distribution, and habitat preference of this animal, which may help to establish stable populations in the future.

Deer*- White Tailed Deer are very plentiful in Southern Illinois. You are most likely to see these critters along road sides or in agricultural fields. Sighting a deer in the woods may be more difficult due to its excellent camouflage. Deer are vocal creatures- If you happen to startle one, it may make a loud snorting noise to alert nearby deer of danger. (Be aware of hunting seasons).

Bats*- There are several species of bats inhabiting Southern Illinois. Prime bat time is at dusk. You may see several darting about, collecting insects. Please be aware that habitat is crucial to their survival.

2. BIRDS: There are approximately 297 species of birds found in Illinois. Of these, 9 species are believed to have been extirpated, and 10 species are threatened or endangered.

Wild Turkey*- The Turkey population is booming in Southern Illinois. Once totally extirpated from the state, efforts to re-establish the turkey population began in 1959. The state developed a trap and transport program which has allowed them to trap turkeys of stable populations elsewhere and transport them to areas with unstable populations. This program has been extremely successful. The best time to sight a turkey would be at dusk or dawn. Know the hunting season and leave your red clothing at home.

Bald Eagle- These birds are most frequently associated with, or can be seen around lakes, rivers, and marshes. For a while, Bald Eagles were endangered due to pesticides present in the fish they were consuming. Although, they have recently been taken off the endangered list and are making a big come back. Crab Orchard Lake is a good place to see these creatures.

Hawks- There are many different types of hawks that inhabit the Southern Illinois area. One that is most commonly sighted is the Red Tailed Hawk. Distinguishing features include a red tail and a white breast, as viewed ventrally (underneath the body). You may spot this bird soaring over open fields or perched in a dead tree, on the look out for food. They are plentiful at Cedar & Draper's Bluffs.

Vultures- An Eagle-sized black bird that can be seen soaring on thermals or updrafts. Vultures are scavengers, feeding mostly on carrion.

Screech Owl*- One of the smaller species of the owl occurring in this area, the screech owl's call has been compared to a woman screaming. If seen in the day, this creature will freeze to protect itself, depending on its camouflage color.

Barred Owl*- It is most commonly distinguished by its call, sounding like the question, "Who cooks for you?" The barred owl lives in thick, lowland forests and it feeds on rodents, birds, frogs, and crayfish.

Whip-poor-will*- Mostly nocturnal, but may be heard at dusk or dawn. Its call is loud and rhythmic, repeating, "Whip-poor-will, whip-poor-will!" It is very rare to sight one of these birds, for they nest on the ground and are extremely well camouflaged. Although, chances are very good that you will hear one. (Purveyors of 2:00 a.m. insanity in your tent- E.U.)

Pileated Woodpecker- The largest of the woodpeckers, this unique creature can be heard uttering its laugh through out the forest, "cuk, cuk, cuk, cuk, cuk." These birds are very elusive and chances are, you may only hear them but never get a glimpse.

3. REPTILES AND AMPHIBIANS: There are approximately 39 species of amphibians and 59 species of reptiles in the state of Illinois.

Copperhead- Viewed from above, this snake has a triangular, coppery-red head and a distinct hourglass pattern on its body. It also has facial pits which are characteristic of pit vipers. Quiet and lethargic in manner, you often find these snakes curled under or lying alongside a log, or sunning on rocks. This snake is poisonous. When alarmed or aggravated, the copperhead will rapidly vibrate its tail. Use caution when around this critter. NOTE: There are some species of water snake that resemble copperheads, but are not poisonous.

Water Moccasin/Cotton Mouth*- When viewed from above this snake is mostly black to greyish in color, with a distinctive triangular head containing facial pits. This snake is poisonous and extreme caution should be used when near it. Its habitat is mostly associated within or near water; it inhabits lakes, streams, rivers and lowlands. Unlike the copperhead, the water moccasin is very aggressive and will stand its ground. When agitated or threatened, this snake is recognizable by presenting it's gapping mouth as a means of defense. Water moccasins are active in day as well as night.

Timber Rattle Snake- Once common in the area, the timber rattler has suffered severe pressure from humans. Its population is in danger now, so the chances of seeing one are slim. The timber rattler reproduces only every other year, which is another cause of population decline. This is a poisonous snake, therefore, caution should be used when near it.

Box Turtle- There are several species of turtle in Southern Illinois. One that is a common terrestrial species is the Box Turtle. This creature has a unique defense method in the form of a shell that will close completely when threatened or alarmed.

Tree Frogs*- These critters may be difficult to spot, hence their excellent camouflage and nature of hanging out in trees. Mostly nocturnal, you may hear a chorus of tree frogs at night. Their calls are similar to that of birds.

Five-lined Skink- The identification of this creature is highly variable depending on age and

Walking Stick- or, is it a sport climber?

sex. Immature skinks display five stripes, with the tail being bright blue (triple A Duracell- E.U.). The adult male and female are usually a duller color, displaying a greyish tail and a red head during mating season. Habitat is normally damp, including rotting stumps, logs, or rock piles. Similar species: Broad-headed Skink.

Fence Lizard- A small, gray or brown spiny lizard, often seen on fence rails, rotting logs, or stumps. They are often spotted sunning themselves on roadsides. They are quick to dash off and seek cover when disturbed.

4. Insects: There are roughly 17,000 species of insects in the state of Illinois! I am presenting a very small fraction of them to you.

Ticks*- Are active at almost all times. After the first couple of frosts in the fall, they are not as readily apparent. When spring warms the land, they appear once again. One of the most common parasites found in the area, living off of the blood of mammals, it is a very hardy creature and may go for weeks without food. It is especially important to check clothing and dogs for presence of these visitors.

Walking Stick*- Hence the name, the Walking Stick bares a striking resemblance to a twig when motionless. Birds are the biggest predators of this creature, which may explain its active manner at night. The color of its immature stages are green, and later become a twig-like brown. See photo this page.

<u>Katydid</u>*- This creature is leaf green in color, inhabiting woodlands. Its favorite food are the leaves of deciduous trees. It is active both in day and night. Its sound is a very loud "katy-DID" chirp.

<u>Ground Bees</u>- If you see them, just steer clear. They will light you on fire.

<u>Black Widows</u>- Are common in the Southern Illinois area. Males are mostly solid black in color, while females have the distinctive red hourglass marking on the abdomen. The female spider is <u>poisonous to humans</u>, while the male is not. A female guarding the egg sac is especially defensive, otherwise she may retreat from disturbances.

<u>Lion Ants</u>- They create the sand traps or "cups" in the sand below cliffs. Then they wait, jaws open, just beneath the base of their trap, ready to chow on unwary critters who fall in. They are also known to throw sand at potential victims, in attempt to knock them into their trap.

<u>Horse & Deer Flies</u>- Males eat pollen and nectar. Females bite mammals. Their saliva contains an antico-agulant. They are attracted to your expired carbon dioxide. (So stop breathing and whining about them, all at the same time- E.U.)

HUNTING

Something to keep in mind is that the Shawnee National Forest is federal land, which means it is man-aged for multiple use. Consequently, many activities other than climbing are permitted. One activity that may be a matter of concern is hunting. It is important to know and realize the hunting seasons. Generally speaking, most hunting seasons, (Deer and Turkey) occur in he Fall: Oct., Nov., Dec. and Jan. As well, spring has April and May hunting seasons. Once again, this is a very general overview of the hunting sea-sons. Be aware that season dates are subject to change annually. For specific information on dates and areas, contact the Illinois Department of Natural Resources Region Five office in Benton at **618-435-8138**.

POISON IVY

Poison Ivy is very common and widespread throughout the forest. If you react negatively to this plant, there are a few things you should know. Poison Ivy is a three leafed, sometimes shiny plant found growing both on the ground and in vine forms on trees. In the fall, the leaves turn a yellow, reddish-orange, or red color. Be aware that you can be affected by Poison Ivy in the winter months, as well. Even if leaves are not present, the vines contain the same irritating oils. So when grabbing that tree for support, be cautious of present vines, especially hairy ones. If contact has been made, wash with soap and water soon!

ABOUT THE AUTHOR:

Debra Eddison holds a B.S. in Zoology, and is currently pursuing graduate education in forestry studies. She has resided in Southern Illinois since 1988. Some of her major inter-ests include wildlife management, habitat man-agement, and forest ecology.

Debra Eddison bouldering at Giant City

Weather*

Many climbers consider Southern Illinois a year-round climbing area, for the most part. Winter can be a surprisingly accommodating season, especially at Draper's Bluff (see Draper's intro). The most favored seasons are spring and fall for their pleasant temperatures, lower humidity, and lack of insects. April clocks in with the lowest average daily humidity levels and unbelievably sticky rock, or is it the shoes? Summers yield their share of mo-skeeters and horseflies big enough to carry away small children and pets. The other main annoyance is what I usually refer to as (for lack of a better term) the little assholes. They're a tiny bee critter that smart when they bite or sting, or whatever it is they do to you. Smacking them usually does no good as they have a hard, rounded shell. You've gotta smack and rub all at once to give them their payback due. That streak of smudge left behind is nothing a little water can't cure. As for summer humidity, consider it a training opportunity. Come dry rock in the fall, you'll feel like a rock ballerina with Ahnold's forearms. If rain is ruining your visit, consider getting a pump at the bouldering cave at the right end of Cedar Bluff. It's probably the last bit of rock to get wet. Cedar and Draper's Bluffs are usually the first places to dry out, especially with a good wind.

Average Humidity %

	6 am	noon	6 pm	midnite
January	82	64	69	77
February	80	61	64	76
March	81	57	58	73
April	78	54	53	70
May	82	56	55	76
June	84	57	56	78
July	86	57	56	78
August	89	57	58	81
September	91	61	64	83
October	84	55	60	76
November	84	62	68	78
December	85	70	75	81

Averages-	Temp. (F) (85 years)	Precipitation (85 years)	Snowfall
January	33.6	3.30"	3.90" (70 yrs.)
February	37.3	2.84"	3.40" (65 yrs.)
March	46.6	4.11"	2.20" (47 yrs.)
April	57.6	4.15"	0.20" (5 yrs.)
May	66.5	4.70"	-
June	75.3	4.04"	-
July	79.1	3.47"	-
August	77.2	4.00"	-
September	70.3	3.54"	-
October	59.1	3.38"	0.10" (3 yrs.)
November	46.7	3.85"	0.70" (22 yrs.)
December	36.9	3.29"	2.40" (56 yrs.)

* Thanks to Jeff Armit, Climatologist at the Southern Illinois Airport, for weather tables.

Numbering System for Climbing Difficulty

Classes are used to assign a general degree of difficulty for going from one point to another.
1st class- walking.
2nd class- hiking, including rough trails.
3rd class- high angle scrambling, hands often used. A rope may be desired.
4th class- easy climbing, but steep enough that hands are usually needed. A rope may be desired.
5th class*- technical free climbing; safety equipment is used to attempt to avoid injury in the event of a fall. Fifth class is broken into difficulty levels, 5.0 to 5.14. The "5" represents 5th class. The number following the decimal point represents the difficulty level. Once 5.9 was surpassed (back whenever), 5.10 became the next level of difficulty, even though it's mathematical nonsense.

For the average person who's in decent shape (huh?), here's a rough explanation of 5th class:

5.0- 5.5	pretty easy stuff.
5.6- 5.7	a little harder than the pretty easy stuff. Many folks start out somewhere around this ability level.
5.8- 5.9	gettin' hard now.
5.10-5.11	even harder. You're approaching uniqueness if you start out at this level.
5.12	advanced.
5.13	you must be training for it.
5.14	Hey moose legs, you don't need to read this. Put on your baggy tights and go open a route so we can hang on it!

Many people drop the "5." when referring to a route's grade. Routes at 5.10 and above are usually further broken into a, b, c, and d subgrades, d being the hardest. The most difficult grades in the world are currently 5.14c/d. The hardest established route in Southern Illinois is currently 5.13b/c.

6th class- Aid climbing. Progress is gained by directly using (e.g.- pulling on) the climbing gear placed in or on the rock.

Grades given to Southern Illinois routes may not necessarily coincide with grades of other areas. More importantly, grades within Southern Illinois are fairly consistent.

I have occasionally been asked, "Why no star system for the good routes?" Here you go:
- It would be my opinion only.
- It's a pain in the arse.
- You figure it out, lazy.
- Quite frankly, most routes would have stars anyway, so let's just call it a 3-Star area instead.

* Necky lead routes are given R and X ratings (see Glossary).

Ethics

For starters, a common comment from the Forest Service is how trash-free climbers seem to be. Let's keep up the lifestyle. Like most climbing communities throughout the U.S. and beyond, the Southern Illinois climbing community has a few self-imposed local guidelines for behavior at the cliffs. They are:

• Leaving a route unattended with gear hanging on it is a bad idea.
• No chipping or use of glue with holds. Reserve it for the climbing gym or your home wall.
• Leave mixed protection routes as such. Restrain from using fixed protection next to adequate natural protection. This is obviously subjective. If you have any doubt, please leave it open for discussion with other climbers who have the ability to place natural protection. How can a "sport-only" climber make an informed decision about whether or not a certain spot will accept a quality gear placement? And, bag the idea that Jackson Falls is just a sport climbing area. It's a <u>climbing</u> area. It contains natural pro routes, top-rope routes, aid routes, sport routes, mixed pro routes, bouldering, & solo (if you want it) routes. Sport routes make up about half (give or take) of existing routes at Jackson Falls.
• Regarding fixed protection:
   "...placement of permanent structures used in climbing and rappelling, including pitons, requires prior approval by the Forest Service... "
   -USDA Forest Service Amended Management Plan, Shawnee National Forest.

Why fixed anchors atop those cliffs, anyway? There are trees everywhere! Well- walk the rim of the Jackson Falls canyon & you'll see that the impact is basically nil. Then go compare that to the top of Shelter One Bluff at Giant City. Enough said.

sign on Rt. 146

Climbing Route Descriptions

Names of climbs are assigned by route authors, not the guidebook author. First ascent (FA) credits have been moved to the route index in the back. Some FA credits were left in the main text to complete the description. Lead protection is listed at the end of each route description. If a route calls for varied pro, bring wedges and cams. Add 2 extra quickdraws to your rack for fixed belay anchors Lead routes in Southern Illinois can be broken into 3 categories:

Routes with natural protection- They'll be listed as <u>natural pro</u>, followed by a general size, such as "small-mid size" or "varied sizes".

Routes with natural and fixed protection- <u>mixed pro</u>, followed by sizes and the number of quickdraws (QD) needed for the fixed pro.

Sport routes- the number of quickdraws will be given. Sport routes will have an <u>underlined</u> title for quick reference.

Critical Info Provided by the Shawnee National Forest and Illinois Department of Natural Resources

The nature of climbing is such that it involves landscapes of relief. In Illinois, these landscapes are confined to the northwest and the southern parts of the state. Because of the rocky, vertical nature of popular climbing spots, many of these areas were spared the disturbance that so many other landscapes received in Illinois. They were too rocky and steep for agriculture; the timber was often inaccessible or too difficult to remove and other developments in these areas were expensive, if not impossible, to effect. As a result, these areas have escaped any significant human impact, have remained relatively intact since Euro-American settlement, and contain natural resources of statewide significance.

Theoretically, all of these unique ecosystems which still exist in the state were identified and catalogued during the Illinois Natural Areas Inventory (INAI). The INAI was a systematic effort to locate, evaluate, describe, and classify these "Natural Areas" for the Illinois Department of Natural Resources (IDNR). These Natural Areas contain a variety of natural communities (assemblages of species which exist in similar environmental and physical circumstances), ranging from wetlands to prairies to forests. The natural communities involving rock exposures have unique plant communities which include sandstone and limestone cliffs and overhangs, sandstone and limestone glades, and mesic, dry-mesic, dry, and xeric upland forests. Many contain endangered and/or threatened plants and animals.

Three of the six areas discussed in this guide are of high enough natural quality to qualify as an Inventoried Natural Area. They are Cedar Bluff, Draper's Bluff and Fountain Bluff. The remaining three (Ferne Clyffe, Giant City and Jackson Falls) were not included on the Inventory and, therefore, little documented information on their natural quality is available. All three inventoried natural areas are located in the Shawnee Hills Natural Division.

Cedar Bluff is recognized for its significant sandstone glades and xeric/dry upland forests. It also has exceptional representative sandstone cliffs and overhangs, and mesic and dry-mesic upland forests. This area has one of the largest acreages (109) of dry/xeric upland forests remaining in Illinois. This forest type is adapted to very harsh, drought conditions and is forested by trees such as post oak (Quercus stellata), blackjack oak (Q. marilandica), black oak (Q. velutina), Chinquapin oak (Q. muhlenbergii), red cedar (Juniperus virginiana), farkleberry (Vaccinium arboreum), and winged elm (Ulmus alata).

The sandstone cliff and overhang communities are characterized by red cedar, various grasses and forbs, lichens, and mosses. These plants exist in pockets of soil in cracks and crevices as well as on the rock substrate.

The mesic and dry-mesic forests contain sugar maple (Acer saccharum), white ash (Fraxinus americana), red oak (Q. rubra), persimmon (Diospyros virginiana), sassafras (Sassafras albidum), catbriers (Smilax spp.), and bluestem grasses (Andropogon spp.).

Draper's Bluff is similar to Cedar Bluff and is located just west of Cedar Bluff. It does, however, lack the dry/xeric forests of Cedar Bluff and its sandstone glade communities are more degraded as a result of grazing and cultivation practices suspected prior to 1938. A significant feature of Draper's Bluff is that it is an outstanding example of a Pennsylvanian escarpment. It also has exceptional examples of sandstone glades and cliffs (similar in vegetation to Cedar Bluff), and mesic and dry-mesic upland forests. The dry-mesic forests are characterized by white oak (Q. alba), red oak and hickories (Carya spp.), while the more mesic forests contain cherrybark oak (Q. falcata var. pagodaefolia), white oak and sugar maple. The natural quality of the dry-mesic forest on privately owned tracts of this natural area has been effected by timber harvest.

Fountain Bluff contains three distinct Inventory Natural Areas, only one of which might be within a climbing area. This area, called Fountain Bluff North, harbors two state endangered species: the allegheny barberry (Berberis canadensis) and the crested coralroot orchid (Hexalectris spicata) and a sandstone cliff community. Also, red honeysuckle (Lonicera dioica var. glaucescens), endangered in Illinois, occurs somewhere at Fountain Bluff; the red honeysuckle is known from only 3 sites in Illinois.

The allegheny barberry is an erect shrub, 1-2 m in height and is extremely rare. It occurs on the rim of the sandstone and is the only known site for this species in the state.

The crested coralroot orchid occurs in the dry upland forest and is a perrenial rhizotamous saprophytic orchid up to

25 cm high. It is known from only a few counties in Southern Illinois.

Eastern woodrats (Neotoma floridana), endangered in Illinois, once occurred at Fountain Bluff on the eastern face but have not been seen in recent years.

Fountain Bluff is largely owned by the Federal Government and managed by the U.S.D.A. Forest Service. However, the Fountain Bluff North INAI containing the two endangered plants is a privately owned tract of Fountain Bluff. Except for the privately owned sections, large parts of Cedar and Draper's Bluff are now owned and managed by the Illinois Department of Natural Resources. Draper's Bluff has a large central core owned by the IDNR but the majority of the desirable climbing bluff faces on the south face and the eastern end of the natural area are privately owned. The northwestern corner of the Natural Area is also privately owned. The western-most tip of the Cedar Bluff INAI and parts of the southeastern exposures are privately owned but the bulk of the Natural Area is in IDNR ownership.

The Forest Service has now completed exchanging Cedar and Draper's Bluff to the Illinois Department of Natural Resources. Regardless of ownership, management objectives remain the same; to protect the significant forest, sandstone glade and sandstone cliff natural communities of the Greater Shawnee Hills Section of the Shawnee Hills Natural Division; to preserve an outstanding geological feature, an example of a Pennsylvanian escarpment. These areas, particularly the sandstone glade and cliff communities, can be quite fragile and can become quickly degraded due to overuse. Care should be taken to avoid their degradation.

As with any other activity, climbing has an impact on the physical environment. The extent of that impact varies with the frequency and duration of that use, the awareness of the user and the physical characteristics of the site. Fortunately, climbers tend to be more environmentally sensitive than many other user groups and, as a result, climbing is sometimes compatible in some environmentally sensitive areas.

Climbing restrictions on various state and federal lands vary and are subject to change. For the most current information on USDA Forest Service land, call or write: Supervisor's Office, 901 S. Commercial, Harrisburg, IL 62946 (618-257-7114). For state property, call or write Region V Conservation Office, P.O. Box 208, Benton, IL 62912 (618-435-8138).

Research Natural Areas in the Shawnee National Forest

Certain areas on the Shawnee National Forest fall under an 8.2 Management Prescription. This Prescription preserves, protects and enhances the unique scientific, educational or natural values found within Research Natural Areas, Geological Areas, Zoological Areas, Ecological Areas, Botanical Areas, and sites listed on the National Register of National Natural Landmarks. Collectively, these areas are known as Natural Areas.

Natural Areas are biologically or geologically unique. They contain a variety of wildlife species and diverse vegetation, predominantly in a natural-appearing condition. Variation in behavior of wildlife species of these sites may range from intolerant to somewhat tolerant of human activities. Existing public use and other human activities range from unnoticeable to very evident. Road networks vary from none to low density.

Ten of the eighty-one Natural Areas in the Shawnee National Forest are Research Natural Areas (RNA's). These ten RNA's total about 5,384 acres. The Shawnee National Forest is a little larger than 265,100 acres in size.

RNA's are part of a national network of field ecological areas designated for research and education and/or to maintain biological diversity on National Forest System lands. RNA's are for non-manipulative research, observation, and study. Sometimes, management such as burning or the removal of exotics, are means by which the RNA's will be maintained in their natural state. RNA's also may assist in carrying out provisions of special acts, such as the Endangered Species Act and the monitoring provisions of the National Forest Management Act. On the Shawnee, the Amended Land and Resource Management Plan (1992) states that recreation uses will be consistent with the protection of area values. Consistent uses are determined by individual site characteristics and usage demands. Recreation use may be prohibited or restricted as necessary to protect the unique features of the area.

Many years of study and work were done by several individuals and agencies, including the Illinois Department of

Conservation, the Illinois Nature Preserves Commission, The Nature Conservancy, the Natural Land Institute, and the Forest Service, in carefully selecting sites for RNA designation in the Shawnee National Forest. National designations of nominated sites on the Shawnee were made between 1989 and 1991. These sites are: Atwood Ridge (955 acres), Barker Bluff (60 acres), Burke Branch (206 acres), Cave Hill (465 acres), Dennison Hollow (205 acres), LaRue-Pine Hills/Otter Pond (2,585 acres), Ozark Hill Prairie (535 acres), Panther Hollow (180 acres), Stoneface (176 acres), and Whoopie Cat Mountain (17 acres).

Two of these RNA's, Cave Hill and Stoneface, have been rock climbing sites for a number of years. With the onset of RNA designation, all ten of these sites have had strict regulations imposed, many of which concern recreational activities such as all terrain vehicle/off highway motorcycle (ATV/OHM) use, equestrian use, hang-gliding, camping, rappelling, and rock climbing. Both Cave Hill and Stoneface have a number of Illinois Threatened and Endangered species which inhabit the many natural communities present.

A species of particular importance is the Mead's milkweed (Asclepias meadii), which is Illinois Endangered and Federally Threatened in the United States. The Mead's milkweed has been the focus of intense research and recovery efforts nation-wide. One of the reasons that rock climbing has been prohibited at Cave Hill and Stoneface is because this species occurs at the top of the cliffs. Over the years, the Mead's populations had dwindled to but a few individuals at these two sites, primarily due to habitat deterioration. Fear of it becoming extirpated from the State prompted numerous institutions and agencies to take action in its recovery effort.

Cave Hill contains relatively undisturbed natural community types of high quality, such as xeric (extremely dry) upland forest, dry upland forest, dry-mesic upland forest, barrens, sandstone glade, and sandstone cliff. There is a cave within the RNA known as Equality Cave (or Cave Hill Cave) that is a significant example of a maze cave in the Interior Low Plateaus Physiographic Province. The cave is also significant for its terrestrial cave community and aquatic cave habitats. The most important features at the Cave Hill RNA are the Mead's milkweed, the old growth forest, the fault-line escarpment, Equality Cave, and the barrens community. The xeric upland forest/dry upland forest/barrens complex that occurs here is the largest of high quality in Illinois. Other significant species include the Illinois Endangered Carolina thistle (Cirsium carolinianum), and the Illinois Threatened chestnut oak (Quercus prinus) and Bradley's spleenwort (Asplenium bradleyi).

Stoneface also contains relatively undisturbed natural community types of high quality. Some of these are xeric upland forest, dry upland forest, dry-mesic upland forest, loess hill prairie, barrens, sandstone glade, and sandstone cliff. Like Cave Hill, Stoneface is geologically significant as a part of a prominent land form, a hogback-like ridge that occurs on a fault-line scarp. This ridge, or cuesta, has sandstone cliffs 100 feet (30.5 meters) high along the scarp face. In addition to the Mead's milkweed, rare plants such as black chokecherry (Aronia melanocarpa) and American orpine (Sedum telephioides) occur on the cliff tops. Also known from this area is the loggerhead shrike (Lanius ludovicianus), Threatened in Illinois.

U.S.D.A. Forest Service
Shawnee National Forest
901 S. Commercial St.
Harrisburg, IL 62946
618/253-7114

The first of these two articles was written by Todd Fink, Naturalist for the Illinois Department of Natural Resources. This reprint is dedicated to his memory. Todd's recent death was a sore blow to friends, family, & colleagues. His expertise had gained extremely wide respect.

Although cooperation was received from the USDA Forest Service and the Illinois Department of Natural Resources, the views expressed throughout this guide may not necessarily coincide with the views of these government agencies.

Fountain Bluff

Fountain Bluff, located at the western edge of the Shawnee National Forest, holds the distinction of having the tallest route in Southern Illinois. Facing northwest, its lack of direct sun until late afternoon provides welcome relief on a hot day, although don't expect to have to take a number. The nearly 200-foot-high bluff isn't known for a heavy traffic of climbers, and rightly so, for aside from one route, the stone is mostly choss. With sections of the wall having names such as The Wall of Manky and The Crispy Face, and route names such as *Zipper* and *Snap, Crackle* and *Pop,* you'll probably appreciate my not giving directions to anything but the one gem route, *Leap Frog.* It sports a jam crack in a roof, so you may want tape. Double ropes are recommended too. Be aware that this particular section of the bluff is on private land. Historically, there has never been any problem between landowners and climbers. Let's keep it that way. Be friendly to all locals and leave the boom box in the car.

Healy and Foster named the route *Leap Frog* because they were apparently one of at least three teams working it. For every attempt made, each party would leave bail gear a bit higher. Carrier and Grosowsky had finally succeeded with the roof, only to be thwarted by the off-width. Their escape via the grassy slab was a feat in itself. The unknown third party was suspected to be from St. Louis. Foster resorted to leading the off-width with no pro. Oogie! In 1986, safety-bolts were installed on lead in the off-width in a moment (hours) of desperation in the dark by Jim Thurmond and myself, Foster's achievement unbeknownst to us.

The Approach

Locate Gorham on the map. Drive into Gorham and turn left onto 2nd Street. Go 2 blocks. As you turn left onto Lake Street, note your odometer. Six-tenths of a mile further should put you right in front of *Leap Frog*. The route has an obvious roof about half-way up the wall. Park on the cliff side of the road. Make sure to locate the descent (see Descent) gully prior to stepping off the road.

LEAP FROG 5.11b

Pitch 1 (5.4)- From the road, locate the shallow, right-facing dihedral about 60' left of the roof and below the ledge. It's more or less a solo so watch for brittle stuff. The tree on the ledge affords a belay for the second if desired. Pitch 2 (3rd class)- Traverse rightward to the belay (bring a big Hex) perch beneath the roof. This is where the route really begins. Pitch 3 (5.11b)- Crank the roof. To avoid a rope-drag nightmare, rig a hanging belay with several (gee, really?) Friends 6 feet or so above the lip of the roof. Pitch 4 (5.10+)- Take the crack to the top. The menacing, overhanging off-width is actually a lie-back for the most part, and it features welcoming safety-bolts. Once on the ledge 10 feet below the top, get psyched for a flaring, off-width exit. There are micro face holds if you look around. Save a #4 Friend for this section. Nobody'll know if you step on it.
FA- Joe Healy, Jim Foster '75

Descent- To rappel, use the tree near the edge 60 feet left (northeast) of the top-out. Use two ropes, obviously, and knot the bottom as they do not reach the ground. Rappel to the 5.4 dihedral (pitch 1). If you're using two 50 meter ropes, you should come within about 20 feet of the ground. Down climb the rest of the way (or simply use 60 meter ropes). To hike down, take the 3rd class gully which is about 500 feet right (south-south-west) of the top-out. Watch for sucker gullies along the way. Joe said that he and Foster spent hours in moon-less dark trying to find the right gully, with nothing else to provide a bearing but the glowing fungi that grow there. OK Joe.

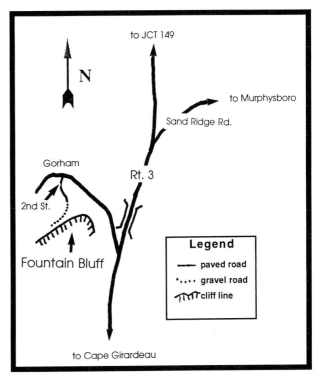

to JCT 149

N

to Murphysboro

Sand Ridge Rd.

Gorham

Rt. 3

2nd St.

Fountain Bluff

Legend

—— paved road

····· gravel road

⊤⋏⊤⊤ cliff line

to Cape Girardeau

Central Southern Illinois Map

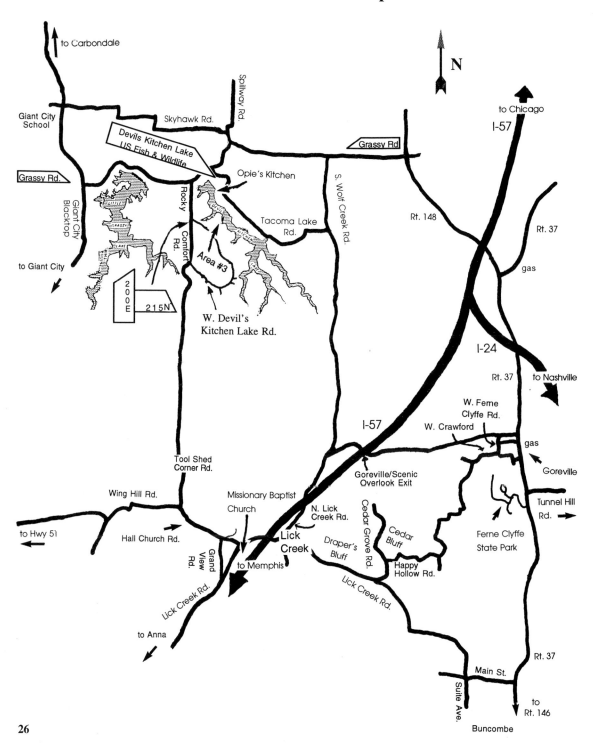

GIANT CITY STATE PARK

Easy to locate on the map, Giant City State Park is located approximately 8 miles south of Carbondale at the end of Springer Ridge Road. The Park features:

- ideal cliffs for beginners and up
- excellent bouldering and top-roping
- a few natural pro leads
- slab to overhang
- paved roads and parking
- campground- showers/electricity
- restaurant/lodge- rental cabins & pool
  618-457-4921
- stables- horse back riding
  618-529-4110

The main climbing areas in the park are Shelter One Bluff (north end) and the Devil's Stand Table area (south end). With the apparent exception of Razor Blade Rock, climbing anywhere else in the park is illegal, especially across the street from Shelter One where there is a fern preserve, Trillium Trail (great trail running). All routes listed for Giant City are top-ropes unless otherwise stated. **For top-rope anchoring at Shelter One Bluff, bring at least 60 feet (twice that for back-up) of anchoring line to reach the trustworthy trees.** Giant City isn't a sport climbing area.

Amenities

Grocery stores, restaurants, hotels and night life are just a few minutes north of the park in Carbondale. If you're wanting to camp for a few bucks a night, there's a campground at the south end of Giant City (see map on page 28). For water, the Ranger Station has an outdoor faucet next to the garage door.

The Giant City Lodge is also at the south end of the park. They have overnight cabins and a restaurant that serves all-you-can-eat yard bird for a decent price. For lunch, the village of Makanda is also worth checking out. See above photo of the historic Makanda Boardwalk.

Giant City State Park

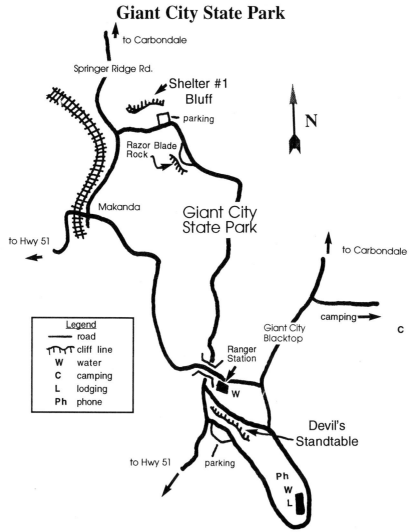

to Carbondale

Springer Ridge Rd.

Shelter #1 Bluff

parking

N

Razor Blade Rock

Makanda

Giant City State Park

to Hwy 51

to Carbondale

camping

C

Legend
— road
⊓⊤⊓⊤ cliff line
W water
C camping
L lodging
Ph phone

Giant City Blacktop

Ranger Station

W

Devil's Standtable

to Hwy 51

parking

Ph
W
L

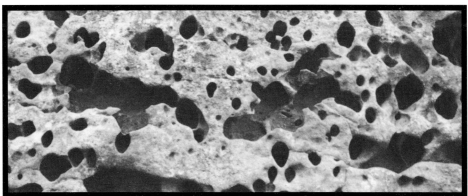

Shelter One Bluff - Giant City

The bluff is behind Shelter One pavilion. Routes in this guide are listed right to left, looking up at the cliff. The trail behind the pavilion accesses the top.

1. **RIGHT SIDE ROUTE** 5.1
High angle step climbing at the far right edge of the bluff.

2. **DRUNKARD'S CRACK** 5.3
Just inside the trees at the right side of the bluff, it's the obvious, wide crack that leads to the top. Commonly soloed to set more difficult routes.

3. **STANDING ON AIR** 5.10
Start at the base of Route #2 & go straight up, using the "nubbettes" to the left of a wash.

4. **SMOOTH CITY** 5.9
Locate Route #5. Ascend the smooth right side of it, skipping the larger holds on the left.

5. **CAMEL'S BACK** 5.5
It's the huge hump above the trailhead that leads rightward to the top. A picnic table is usually right in front of the route. Begin at the right of the hump and climb up toward the center. Top out through vertical bucket climbing.

6. **RETURN TO FOREVER** (pretty hard bouldering)
A pumpin', non-crimpin', world class traverse- start at the base of Route #4 and traverse to the bottom of *Poison Ivy* (#29) or vice-versa.

7. **FULL MOON FOOT DANCE** difficult no hands route
Start beneath Route #5 (crux is right off the ground) and work up and right. Top out through Route #2 (top move is death) or angle up to Route #1.

8. **THE GULLY** 5.5
Start under Route #5 & traverse leftward to the obvious gully. Top out slightly left.

9. **MONKEY MOVE** 5.9
Climb to the safety-bolt on the bulge just left of Route #8.

10. **HUMIDITY DIRECT** 5.11b
Climb the face 5 feet left of Route #9. Avoid the big crack to the left (Route# 12).

11. **HUMIDITY** 5.10ish (boulder moves)
Go up Route #12 for about 10 feet. Traverse rightward onto Route #9's bulge.

12. MAKANDA LAYBACK 5.8

It's the obvious, wide crack that defines the beginning of the cliff's overhung section. At the top of the wide crack, step right & go up to the safety-bolt. From there, go left to a small, triangular ledge. Go straight up & top out left of the small tree. Fairly committing lead- small-mid pro.

13. TEMPURATOUR 5.7 (classic lead route)

<u>Pitch 1</u>- Climb Route #12 to the safety-bolt (small nut will back it up) and belay. <u>Pitch 2</u>-Traverse left to the belay ledge above Route #21. <u>Pitch 3</u>- go up 10-15 feet and traverse leftward to *Poison Ivy* gully (Route #27) . Down climb about 10 feet and traverse left to Route #36. <u>Natural pro</u>- varied sizes

variation (5.7)- down climb about 10 feet from the belay ledge, traverse left to *Poison Ivy* gully & go up or continue to the top of Chimney (#36) for a hanging belay.

sick variation (5.9)- traverse all the way to Route #41.

14. OPEN BOOK 5.7

Climb through the wide crack of Route #12, then traverse straight left to the large, open book gully & go up it.

15. ELECTRIC KOOL-AID ACID TEST 5.11

Start on Route #12 and angle slightly leftward. Stay only 3-5 feet left of the crack (Route #12). Ascend the blank face 20 feet up. Once on good holds, pick your line.

FA- Joe Healy, Jim Foster 70's, then the key, tiny knob broke off and Foster nabbed the new FA (*Knobless*). **variations** (5.11)- There are 2 or 3 a bit left. Avoid #16's bowling ball pocket.

16. OPEN BOOK DIRECT 5.9

Start at the base of Route #12. Angle up and left to the bowling ball pocket. Top out through the open book gully.

17. THACKERY'S WACKERY 5.12 (boulder moves)

At the base of Route #12, match hands on the bucket 4 feet off the ground. With your feet inches from the ground, traverse 10 feet left & go straight up into Route #16's bowling ball pocket.

18. RAPPELLERS' DEMISE 5.11

Start at the 2 baseball sized, stacked pockets, about 15 feet left of Route #12. The route has an upside-down V-formation about 5 feet left of Route #16's bowling ball pocket. Climb through the upside down V-formation.

19. CRACKPOT 5.11

About 5 feet to the left of Route #18, it's the obvious overhanging crack equipped with neighboring face holds to the left. Right hip jam at top of crack for a unique, no-hands rest. Top out the overhang through the obvious, little cave straight above. The little cave has a styling, drop-hands right knee lock in it.

FA- Jim Foster during snowfall 70's

1st Free Lead- Chris Ecklund with psycho-pro '88

20. MY FEET ARE SMILING 5.11
About 12 feet left of Route #19, start with the neck sized pinch. Head 10 feet up & right through the 2-foot, peanut shaped dish which is about 15 feet off the ground. From there, work up & left to a 6-inch, right heel-hook-swallowing-horizontal-ledge. Then climb through the honeycomb section up & right. Same little cave top-out a Route #19.
FA- Doug Drewes, Joe Healy 70's Leo Kottke fans

21. GRAVES 5.10 R (grävz)- a B & G wine from the Graves district- has a limestone overtone due to the rocky ground where the grapes were grown.) Same neck grab start as Route #20. Climb up & slightly left to the horizontal hand-slot that takes pro (that's all you get 'til the cave!). Then head up to the lieback holds up & right. Go up & left to the cave. From the cave, traverse 15 feet up and left to the small gully, then go straight up to a nice belay ledge with a safety-bolt and pin. From the ledge, angle up and right to the top. <u>Natural pro</u>- varied sizes (probably never led w/out TR rehearsal)
variation (5.10 TR)- from the cave, angle up and right to the *Crackpot* (#19) cave.

22. I'M A BITCH 5.12a
Start on Route #21. Immediately move up and left about 4 feet. Continue straight up, avoiding *Graves'* (#21) obvious, horizontal hand-slot. Top out the overhang through *Dim View* (#23).

23. DIM VIEW / NIGHT OF THE LIVING DEAD 5.12a
Start on the "match-hands" bucket about 5 feet right of Route #25 (or 10 feet left of Routes 20 & 21). Go up & left, paralleling the dihedral crack (Route #25). At the first big horizontal, go straight up.
FA- Doug Drewes, Joe Healy, Jim Foster 70's Foster originally soloed it to the crux in the dark, but apparently thought better.

Ken Vanstone boulders below Alan Carrier doing an "L-sit" on *Graves*, Giant City State Park

David Curtis on *Makanda Layback*, Giant City State Park

24. **WATERLOO** 5.11
Start between Routes #23 & 25. It's a long, reach move start to a flat-bottom pocket. Continue straight up. Avoid the dihedral to the left and Route #23's starting bucket. Hope you're taller than Napoleon.

25. **JILL'S** 5.11
It's the obvious dihedral crack directly above the sizeable boulder in the ground.

26. **CITY LIMITS** 5.12+
Overhanging pocketed face just left of *Jill's* dihedral (Route #25). Starts on great holds. After the slab rest, pull the overhang up above also. Just try to flash it on-sight. Futuristic pocket pulling for its time. **FA-** Joe Healy, Jim Foster. After several months of attempts, including barefoot "toe-hooking" experimentation, they finally succeeded in E.B.'s.

Poison Ivy **gully is the first, large gully to the right of the woods that starts 20+ feet off the ground and continues to the top.**

27. **POISON IVY RIGHT** 5.9
About 10 feet left of Route #25, take the big dihedral/lieback left-ward into the *Poison Ivy* gully. <u>Natural pro-</u> varied sizes **variation-** prior to moving into the gully, cut rightward through the iron flake/pocket. Stay left of #26.

28. **POISON IVY CENTER** 5.10
Start directly under the *Poison Ivy* gully and go straight into it.

29. **POISON IVY** 5.9
About 5 feet left of Route #28, a series of very positive leftward lieback moves allow you to head rightward into the bottom of the *Poison Ivy* gully.

30. **DOUBLE BARREL** 5.11

Begin 5 feet left of Route #29's leftward lieback start. Climb up through the two large pockets just left of the base of *Poison Ivy* gully. Avoid using the gully. Continue straight up.

31. **NO VACANCY** 5.11+

Really just a contrived variation of Route #30. Start 2-3 feet left of Route #29. Go straight up, using only the left of Route #30's two large pockets.

32. **SHOTGUN** 5.11

Same start as Route #30. Head up and left through the short, but obvious lieback crack that goes through the overhang. Continue the same direction through small pockets.

33. **WALK UP** 5.10

About 18 feet left of Route #29, start on the vertical lieback crack. Go straight up through a break in the overhang that takes you under an obvious white stripe. Lieback moves up and right lead you to the top-out.

At the edge of the woods to the left, locate the steep overhang just off the ground. A pretty darn hard bouldering traverse, *The Undoable,* goes across the lip of the overhang.

34. **DEAD DOG** 5.10+

Start at the thin crack at the lip of the above mentioned *The Undoable.* Climb through the small crack systems for nearly 40 feet. Traverse slightly rightward and top out through the overhangs.

35. **THE IDIOT** 5.11

Start 8 feet left of Route #34, just to the right of a tree. Go up about 20 feet, then traverse up and right for 30 feet more, crossing Route #34. Then traverse up and left 30 feet. Exit through iron flakes near a small cedar tree.

36. **CHIMNEY** 5.5

It's the obvious giant chimney just inside the woods. Start at its bottom left crack. Large natural pro. **variation-** start at the point where your TR line hangs & go straight up into the chimney.

37. **SHAKE AND BAKE** 5.9

Start at Route #36. Ascend the upper crack system just left of *Chimney*.

38. GEORGE'S NOSE 5.10+
Start at Route #36. Go straight up, all
the way through the overhung nose up
above.

39. GEORGE'S 5.7
Do the 1st half of Route #38. At the
overhang, step up left into the chim-
ney/crack. Take it to the top.
variation (5.7)- Start on Route #41.
Half way up, traverse rightward across
the slab to the chimney/crack. Been
lead before. <u>Natural pro</u>- varied sizes

40. THE BULGE 5.10
Start on the 8-foot tall rightward lieback
about 10 feet left of Route #36. Pull
the mantel shelf 10 feet up. Then go
straight up to the top, staying 6 feet left
of Route #39's upper chimney/crack.

41. JOE'S VARIATION 5.8
Start near the tree, about 25 feet left of
Route #36. Ascend the left facing pseu-
do-crack system straight above. <u>Natural
pro</u>- varied sizes (for a bold one).
FA- Joe Dittamore 70's Local lore says
that Joe disappeared sailing off the
coast of South America- pirates per-
haps?

42. BOB'S VARIATION/HIP POCKET 5.9
Take Route #41 for about 20 feet. Traverse leftward for about 5-10 feet and go up to the smooth,
overhanging bulge. Crank though the lone, 3-finger pocket and go straight up.
FA- Bob Milburn, Chris Franks 70's Prior to his death, Bob had gone from rodeo life to being
an outstanding veterinarian.

43. NOWHERE 5.10
About 10 feet left of Route #41, take the small, overhang start to the pentagonal hand-pocket. Go
straight up to a slab step-shelf. Top out straight through the overhanging second half.

44. BARNES' OVERHANG 5.9
At the top of the trail's slope, about 25 feet left of Route #43, ascend the slab to the short, overhanging bulge with honeycomb-like pocket features.

45. **EASY CRACK** 5.4
Ascend the obvious, broken crack system 10 feet left of Route #44. Top out at the cedar tree.
<u>Natural pro</u>- mid-big sizes

Continue leftward on the trail for about 120 feet. You'll come to a seasonal waterfall.

46. **WATERFALL SLAB** 5.3
It's the long, easy slab to the right of the aforementioned waterfall.

Razor Blade Rock

Razor Blade Rock is next to the road a few hundred yards south of the Shelter One parking lot. Park at the narrow lot across from the large field, just south of the Stonefort Trail sign. The bouldering spot is the short, slightly overhung face, right across the creek on the west side of the road. All of the moves exit onto a large shelf. Traverse rightward to the crack to descend. Also, a fairly extreme traverse crosses the bottom of the wall.

Kathy Hope on Razor Blade Rock

Devil's Stand Table area (south end)

Main bouldering area

Although I've listed only 6 routes for this area, there are other quality TR's. For lack of route names and FA's, I've left it to you to eyeball everything else. The trail starts across the street from the northernmost end of the Devil's Stand Table parking lot. At the intersection of the trail and the bottom of the bluff, you'll be facing *The Gully*.

1. THE GULLY 5.3
See previous paragraph.

2. NAME UNKNOWN 5.7
It's the crack that starts 15 feet to the left of Route #1.

Continuing leftward from the *Name Unknown* crack is a 10-foot high roof equipped with taxing boulder problems. An easy leftward traverse to a gully/crack provides an exit. Quality bouldering abounds all along the cliff.

3. JACK'S CRACK 5.7
It's the crack at the left edge of the bouldering roof.
FA- Probably Jack

Matthew Tender Lovin' Brotherton IV

John Sommerhof on *One, Two, Three*

4. **ONE, TWO, THREE** 5.8
About 60 feet left of *Jack's Crack* (#3), it's the crack with a triple overhang system. Protects well for leading. <u>Natural pro-</u> varied sizes

Devil's Standtable

5. THE SCOUT 5.0

When walking in from the parking lot, turn **right** at *The Gully* (#1) & go about 110 feet, just beyond the rise in the path to the clean and easy slab.

6. STANDTABLE ROUTE 5.8

Several hundred feet to the right of route #5, a park service sign marks the Devil's Standtable. Climb the face directly behind the sign. It tops out through a small overhang.

Leif Faber (heel hooking)

Mandy Harrison & Wiley

Devil's Kitchen Lake

On opposite sides of Devil's Kitchen Lake are two quality bouldering areas known as Area #3 and Opie's Kitchen (larger area). See Central Map on page 26 for directions. Specific boulder moves are yours to find.

Area #3

A must hit on the bouldering circuit, Area #3 offers several roof moves, afternoon sunshine, and a fun and easy traverse over the water. Don't fall in though as swimming is illegal in DK Lake. If a ranger sees you wet, you'll get nailed for 50 bucks.

Take the 3rd left as you drive in. You'll see a "3" on the back of a stop sign. Drive on back & park at the circle. Take the short trail leading southwest to the water's edge. The roof is right there. The easy traverse heads leftward.

Andy Boone bouldering at Area #3 while Oscar contemplates an illegal swim

Opie's Kitchen

Opie's Kitchen holds a wealth of excellent bouldering ranging from fun & easy stuff to overhanging nightmares. Some of the boulders make for ideal TRing with entry level kids under ten. Sitting on top & giving a body belay is quick & easy. Park at the Rocky Bluff parking lot as denoted on the map. Locate the trail beginning across the road from the Rocky Bluff Trail Head. Hoof along the faint trail toward the spillway which skirts the top of a short bluff for about 500 feet. Descend the 1st easy walk-down through a narrow hallway (option- continue on top to an easier step down). Continuing below, just past a short slope, you'll come to the 90-100 foot, slightly overhanging traverse that sports some really cool pinches. It has a high, middle, & low traverse. The first big boulder to your right is Girlfriend Rock. The sun hits you late in the day.

Kerby McGhee chewin' up *Dora's Monster Brisket*

Opie's Kitchen

Girlfriend Rock

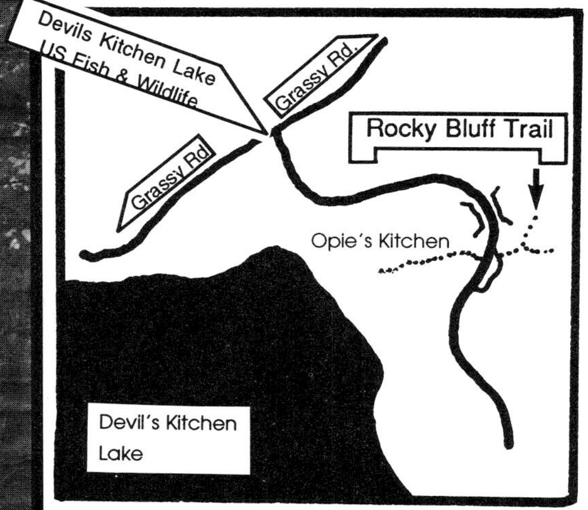

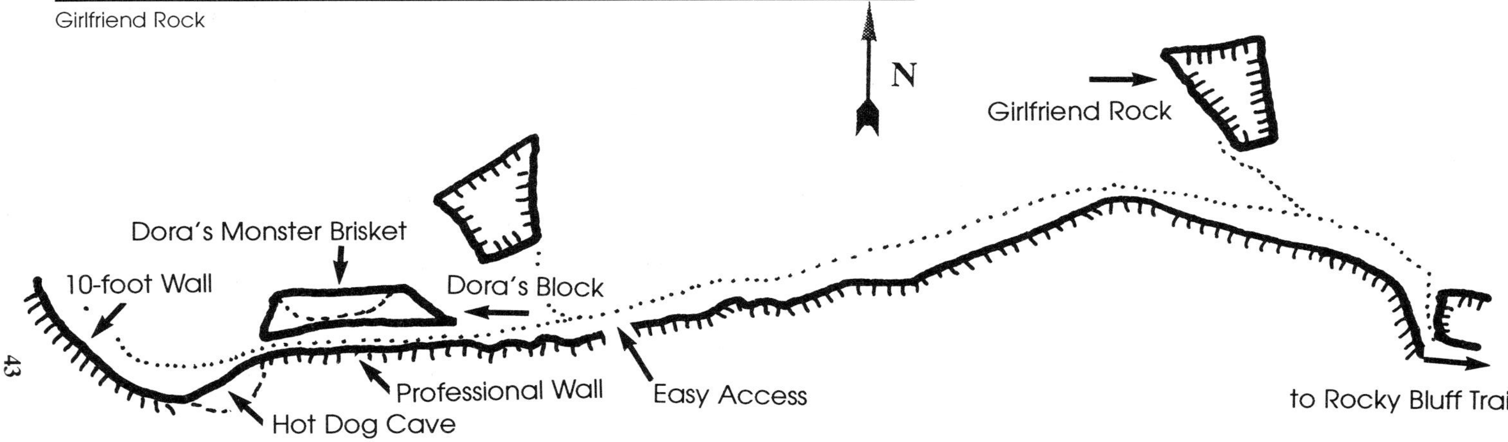

to Rocky Bluff Trail

Girlfriend Rock

N

Easy Access

Dora's Block

Professional Wall

Hot Dog Cave

Dora's Monster Brisket

10-foot Wall

Rocky Bluff Trail

Opie's Kitchen

Grassy Rd.

Grassy Rd.

Devils Kitchen Lake
U.S. Fish & Wildlife

Devil's Kitchen Lake

43

CEDAR BLUFF

Cedar Bluff stands 80-90 feet tall above a forested ridge. On a sunny day, one can sit on top of the southwest-facing cliff and take in the 30+ mile view of rolling meadows scattered with farmhouses. The routes on the half-mile long cliff tend to be mostly vertical, with an occasional steep section or roof. Over a dozen routes are at or below 5.10 and setting up a top-rope is easy on every one of them. All routes listed for Cedar Bluff are leadable unless otherwise noted.

The summer sun is usually pretty brutal, making Cedar Bluff (and Draper's) an ideal spot to hit from October through May. The ticks in the summer can also get pretty obnoxious. Worse yet, the Draper's Bluff approach seems to have more.

The trail up to Cedar Bluff used to be a road leading to the Cedar Grove School at the base of the cliff. The foundation and water well are all that remain. Hence, the Playground Wall with *Detention* and *Let's Play Doctor.*

The Illinois Department of Natural Resources has acquired possession of Cedar Bluff (except for the privately owned section). It is now part of Ferne Clyffe State Park. Check with Ferne Clyffe about the status of primitive camping prior to pitching your tent at the bluff. They may even post new regulatory signs.

Amenities

For food and water, go 5 or 6 miles eastward on Lick Creek road to Buncombe. Hang a left on Main Street and go 2 blocks. Hillside Convenience sits at the intersection with Highway 37. They sell liquor and a few groceries. For gas, a more complete shopping experience, Dad's Pizza or Dairy Barn, head about 5 miles north of Buncombe on 37 to Goreville (see map on page 50 for direct back road to Goreville from the cliffs). For a campground with a shower for a few bucks a night, there's Ferne Clyffe State Park. It's about a mile or 2 shy of Goreville heading north on 37. Marion (20 minutes from Cedar Grove Church) and Carbondale (35 minutes) have the largest concentration of motels/hotels and restaurants.

Reminiscence with Jim Hancock

The following was obtained in an interview with 75-years-young Jim Hancock, Buncombe resident.

I was born in 1920. I went to Cedar Grove School. The school was built out of milled poplar. It had a wooden shingle roof. The school had about 50 wooden desks, each with an ink well. You had to dip your quill about every five words. We had first through eighth grades all together in the one room. That trail up there use to be the wagon road that went to the big cave. That's where our teacher use to tie his horse up. The rest of us walked to school every day.

We heated the building with coal. That low overhang in the rocks right up there behind the school house served as the coal house. When the state inspector would come around, he'd just mark the coal house as being very sturdy and well built. Why- I bet you could still find some coal under that overhang if you looked close enough.

When was it closed? Well let's see. Vic, my son- he was born in '47. He went to the first grade there, so it must have been around 1954 or '55 when they closed it and tore it down. Right before the land was sold to the state, someone stole the school bell out of the belfry. How they got it off and out of there I'll never know. It weighed about 500 pounds.

Now you know that the school house was originally up on top of the cliff don't you? It was up there on the northeast side. They actually moved it piece by piece to the bottom. When? Oh, it must have been about 1910, because my father went there for a while before it was moved. Why? I think they thought it was dangerous for the kids going to and from school. Anyone ever hurt you say? Yes, it was Cletus Barringer's daughter. Can't remember her name- was before my time. Anyway, her brothers decided they would lower her off the cliff with a rope, about 200 feet east of the school house. She must have been about 30 feet or so still above the ground when they ran out of rope. What'd they do? They dropped her- that's what they did, and she died. A real shame it was.

Did we ever climb around? The teacher's hickory rod kept us off those rocks- that was two-year-old hickory. Kids behaved more back then. You see, we didn't have outhouses. The girls' bathroom was behind that one rock with the little cave behind it down below the school house. The boys would sometimes, you know, see what they could if they climbed the bluff a ways- if they dared. Yes, I remember the hickory rod. Now, the boys went to the bathroom by the big cave where the teacher tied up his horse.

Did we climb around before school? Well the teacher was always there when we got there. After school? Heh heh. Why- we went home and worked! I do remember on occasion having climbed up and down that big crack in the rock above the big ledge right behind the school house. That rock up there is sandstone you know. It's got those holes in the rock- I always called them pockets. I don't know what you refer to them as. Oh, you do, too? Those would be good for grabbing onto...

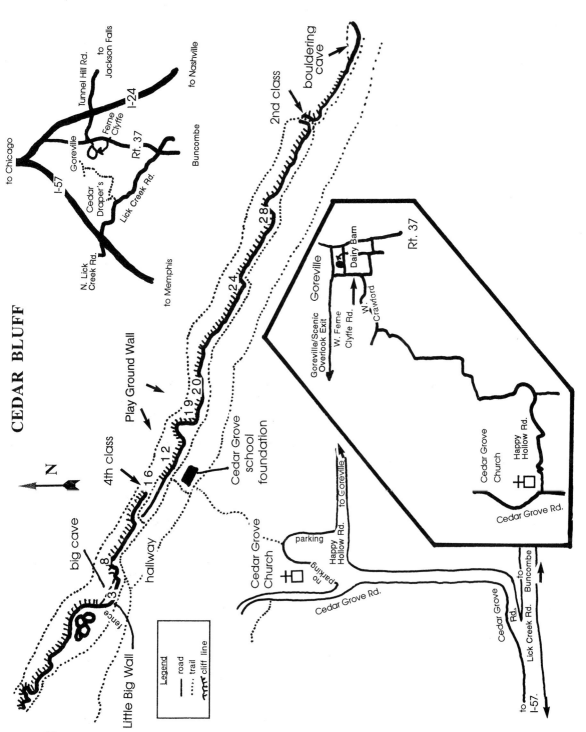

CEDAR BLUFF

The Approach

Cedar and Draper's Bluffs are located approximately 15 miles south of Marion and 3 miles east of I-57 on Lick Creek road. As you travel east of Lick Creek, you'll drive by the length of Draper's Bluff. Skip parking along the road. Keep going (about 3 miles from I-57) and turn left at Cedar Grove Road. Drive .8 mile to the church. Park your car on the lower right half of the parking lot next to the church (state park property). The left (upper) half of the lot is owned by the church. Please refrain from making noise during church services, using the outhouse behind the church, and camping at the parking lot. The traditional method of signifying your where-abouts to your partners is to point your vehicle toward your bluff of choice, Draper's or Cedar.

The 5 minute trail to Cedar Bluff begins at the edge of the woods behind the church. Further up the hill, it intersects with a trail which parallels the bluff line (there also are trails which fol-low the entire bluff's contour along both the bottom and top of the cliff). Forty yards to the left of the intersection is the big Cave. There is a fence at the left edge of the big Cave which blocks access to the left end of the bluff. Please respect the landowner's right to privacy- DO NOT cross the fence. If you do, you'll jeopardize SICA's and the Access Fund's possibilities of negotiating with the landowner.

The Little Big Wall

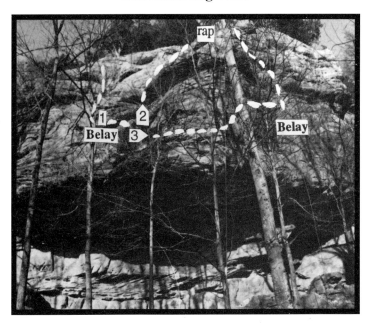

Step back from the front of the big Cave and look up at the lower left part of the upper wall. Spot the fixed belay station at a grassy ledge. It serves Routes #1,2, & 3. Wild blackberries grow on the ledge for summer diehards. To access it, rappel from a fixed anchor just below the top of the upper wall. Knot the end of your 50m rope as it won't reach the ground.

Routes starting above the big Cave on The Little Big Wall

1. **MOVING RIGHT ALONG** 5.10a or 5.7
See previous paragraph. From the belay ledge, traverse leftward 15 feet and go up to the safety-bolt at the base of a gully. Ascend the left side of the gully and go straight over the bulge to the top. Mixed pro- varied sizes and 1 QD
variation (5.7)- stay with the crack at the top of the 2nd pitch.

2. **SAMPSON** 5.9
Short, but kinda fun. Start at the belay station. Go straight up from the belay through the center of a gully. A safety-bolt above the upper lip protects the crux move. A long, easy slab tops it out. Mixed pro- varied sizes and 1 QD

3. **PIONEERS AND CONNOISSEURS** 5.11
Pitch 1 (5.11)- From the belay ledge, traverse rightward (bring TCU's) around the corner to the first safety-bolt. A funky, upward reach move takes you to the second safety-bolt. Continue about 25 feet rightward across a ledge system to a fixed, hanging belay. Pitch 2 (5.7)- Mantel above the belay and look up and right for the last safety-bolt. Angle up & left to the top. Mixed pro- TCU's, Friends, 2 QD + anchor
variation For a fun 5.7, rappel directly to the second pitch belay and climb out. Knot your rope end as it DOES NOT reach the ground.
another variation (5.7) From the hanging belay, keep traversing to *Dizzy* (#4).

Back on the Ground...

4. **DIZZY** 5.12a (super fun roof) or 5.8
Pitch 1 (5.7 or 5.10a)- Start at the first major dihedral (Route #5) 15 feet to the right of the big Cave (Jim Thurmond opted to solo the [nasty landing] horizontal dihedral out of the cave for the start). After the 1st clip (prior to it, a small stopper & mid-size Friend help remove the deck factor), traverse leftward out on the face. The third safety-bolt can either be the far left one (5.10a) or the one straight up (5.7). Ascend up and slightly left to the belay anchor. Pitch 2 (5.12a)- Traverse rightward to the safety-bolt under the roof. Crank the roof! 3 more QD take you up the arete to the fixed anchor. Route can be done in 1 pitch- long runner under the roof. Doubled 50m rope reaches the ground. 8 QD + anchor.
Pitch 2 variation (5.8) Skip the roof by climbing above the belay anchor through the gully to a safety-bolt. Climb up and rightward onto the arete above the roof, then go to the anchor.

Bill Jones on *Dizzy*, Cedar Bluff

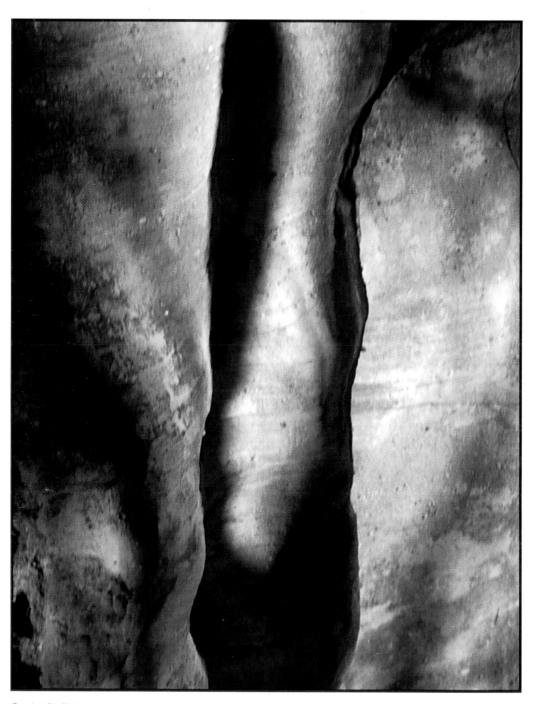

Cedar Bluff stone

5. UNFINISHED SYMPHONY 5.10a

<u>Pitch 1</u> (5.8)- Climb the dihedral (same start as #4) to where it cuts rightward. Go around the corner and rig a hanging belay. <u>Pitch 2</u> (5.10a)- Ascend the ramp/dihedral to a safety-bolt and top out on edges out left. Originally rated 5.8/A4 until Sean Scuras and Clay Erickson installed the safety-bolt on the 2nd pitch to make it go free in 1984. A classic.

<u>Mixed pro</u>- varied sizes and 1 QD- Friends help

6. <u>SEAMS HARD</u> 5.12b

Continue up the slope from Route #5 for about 25 feet. Ascend the sport route with the lieback seam above the 1st clip. It starts about 7 feet <u>left</u> of the obvious off-width (Route #7). 6 QD + anchor.

Pleasure Sequence variation (5.12b)- Begin 10 feet left of *Seams Hard*. Face climb up and right to meet *Seams Hard* at the lieback seam.

7. FEAR OF FLYING 5.9
The ugh looking off-width next to Route #6.
1st Free Lead- Bob Ward, Greg Clark '81 Bob used a measuring tape on lead and called the dimensions to Greg, who promptly sawed the 2x4's to size for Bob to haul up for pro.

8. CAVE CITY 5.6
Ascend the obvious dihedral/corner just right of *Fear of Flying*. Fairly long & very fun.
<u>Natural pro</u>- varied sizes. Better feel comfy leading 5.6. A whipper on this would get ugly fast.

9. <u>2 SIX-PACKS, 1/5 OF SCOTCH & A FULL MOON</u> 5.12a
Begin 30 feet right of *Cave City* (#8). Vertical to slab climbing for 20 feet takes you to a semi-clean overhanging face. Climb just left of a 6-foot pillar with a flat top. Once on top of the pillar, take the line of least resistance to the top. 4 QD + anchor.
FA- Jim Thurmond, Pete Story (doin' the late night thang) '88

Approximately 100 feet to the right of Route #8 is an obvious, narrow hallway that takes you to a large ledge which serves as the exit to Routes 10-14 on the Playground Wall. An easy to find, 4th class scramble from the ledge provides access to the top of the cliff.

PLAYGROUND WALL

10. AFRICA 5.8 TR
Start 10 feet *left* of Route #11. Climb straight up the flakes (one of which resemble the continent), directly beneath the tree on the ledge.
<u>Natural pro</u>- basically a solo.

11. DETENTION 5.10a
Start 10-15 feet *left* of Route #12.
<u>Mixed pro</u>- 2 QD, mid Hex or Friend. Better know how to place gear on this one.

12. MIKE'S MEANDER 5.5
About 100 feet rightward from the hallway/walk-up entrance, it's the first, slightly overhanging and horn-filled crack that faces a large clearing. Walk-off leftward on the ledge. Has been an impeccable 1st lead for many. <u>Natural pro</u>- varied sizes.
Pitch 2 (5.9 seldom done)- Directly above the anchor for Routes #13/14, ascend the overhanging crack for about 20 feet, traverse leftward 8 feet, then continue up the crack to where it tops out a bit right. <u>Natural pro</u>- varied sizes.

13. **ITTY BITTY TITTIES** 5.12a

Sport route 15 feet *right* of Route #12. After clipping the first pin, clip the safety-bolt for your third piece. Ascend straight from there. 5 QD + anchor.

14. **LET'S PLAY DOCTOR** 5.11d

Variation of Route #13- clip the 2nd pin for your third piece. 5 QD + anchor.

15. **HIGH FLYING BIRD** 5.8

About 20-25 feet right of Routes #13/14, ascend the face up to a narrow crack that splits the overhang & brings you to the right end of the ledge.

Mixed pro- 2 QD, mid sizes + anchor

16. **NUMBER 35** 5.9

Short route that can serve as a second pitch to Routes #11-14. It starts on the ledge about 10 feet left of the 4th class scramble to the top. 2 QD

17. **SHORT STUFF** 5.11a TR

Short face route that starts on the ledge about 8 feet right of the 4th class scramble to the top.

18. **NO NAME** 5.9 TR

Start 10 feet to the right of Route #17 on the vertical crack at the left end of the steep overhang. Go straight up.

Natural pro- varied sizes

Back on the ground and continuing rightward from Routes 13/14...

19. **SCHOOL YARD BLUES** 5.11a

First sport route around the corner. A true beauty. Fun roof for final moves. 5 QD + anchor

20. **GHOSTS AND GOBLINS** 5.10a
It's about 100 feet to the right of Route #19. The route goes up a large, partial-pillar/arete, to the right of which is a prominent gully. FA went on Halloween. Don't get spooked!
Mixed pro- 3 QD, small-mid pro + anchor

21. **COMMUNITY PROPERTY** 5.9
Ascend the crack system in the gully just right of Route #20. Top out straight.
Natural pro- varied sizes
variation (5.7)- Traverse left under the upper headwall at the top for the exit.

22. **BIG STING** 5.9
It's about 30 feet to the right of Route #21. Use the tree to access the slab. Ascend the easy slab to the obvious, right-facing dihedral crack in the small roof. Go to the gully and top out to the left. Jeff stirred the wasps, John made 'em mad and Brian got nailed.
Natural pro- varied sizes
FA- Jeff Scheff, John Payne, Brian Vana '85

23. <u>**DOS EQUIS**</u> 5.9+
About 75 feet right of *Big Sting* (#22), go up the first sport route at the corner. Two natural X features just above the first clip mark the route. Start above a low roof. 5 QD + anchor

24. **THOMAS BEAR MEMORIAL** 5.11a
Just right of #23, climb the middle of the large face left of a big dihedral/gully.
Mixed pro- varied sizes, 3 QD + anchor
FA- John Payne '88 bad-ass climb named after John's bad-ass cat. Feeling adventurous? Skip the first 2 clips to emulate the FA.

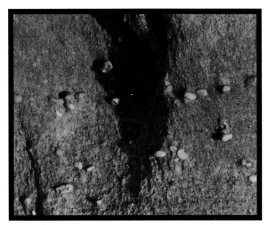

25. <u>**JACK IN THE GREEN**</u> 5.13a
Sport route that ascends the slab/face opposite from *Thomas Bear* (#24). Scamper up next to the tree (use it, so what) 12 feet left of the route line and traverse into the route. Climb the heinous slab (hee hee) to the base of the overhanging arete. Good luck. Clip the pin (#26) in the slanted dihedral (long runner) and ascend the upper arete. 10 QD + anchor. Come on you sport folks. This route could use a 2nd ascent. **Direct bouldering start-** Brutal reach move below 1st clip. If I could just dislocate my shoulder a little more...

Keith Adams on *Dos Equis*

26. HYPOTHERMIA 5.10a

<u>Pitch 1</u> (5.8)- Just right of Route #25, ascend the gully up to the base of the arete and belay.
<u>Pitch 2</u> (5.10a)- Traverse the dihedral crack up & left to the next gully and belay at the tree. 4th class out or rappel from tree. <u>Mixed pro</u>- varied sizes, 1 pin
FA- John Payne, Greg Simmons early winter '86 After leading the 1st pitch & rigging a belay, John nearly froze his arse off belaying Greg up & through the 2nd pitch.

27. THE LATS WALTZ 5.12b
About 50 feet right of Route #26, ascend the easy looking, shallow gully above a low roof. 9 QD + anchor. Go ahead- Make 'em dance.

28. ST. LOUIS GRAFFITI 5.11d
It's the first sport route around the corner., right of #27. Route ends at 1st shelf. 3 QD + anchor.

29. OILY EASTER BEAVER 5.12a
Sport route just right of Route #28. 5 QD + anchor.

30. **APRIL FOOL** 5.10a R
Left-facing dihedral beginning 5 feet right of *Oily Easter Beaver* (#29).
<u>Natural pro</u>- varied sizes + same anchor as (#29).
FA (on-sight)- John Payne

31. <u>**VOGUE**</u> 5.12a/b
Ascend the face 15 feet right of *April Fool* (#30). 6 QD + anchor.

32. **COOL DOWN** 5.8
Locate the dihedral in the corner, just right of *Vogue* (#31). Ascend the cleanest section of face to the right of the dihedral. <u>Mixed pro</u>- varied sized, 2 QD + anchor
FA (on-sight)- John Payne, amped with endorphins after leading the FA of *April Fool* on-sight.

Less than 100 yards further right is a casual walk-up gully to the top. Just to the right of it is the Bouldering Cave. It's a great place to get a pump, especially if the weather is raining on your parade.

Bouldering Cave

John Payne lays it out in the Bouldering Cave

DRAPER'S BLUFF

to
Cedar Grove
Church

N

Loony Bin

2nd class
gully

fence

1

2

3

1

2

8

12

15

Rubik's Cube

24 20

28

camping ledge

3rd class gully

30

33

36

39

Tomato Rock

45

48

51

A-Corner

58

cattle cave

59

fence

3rd class
gully

Rubik's Cube

Camping Ledge

Tomato Rock

A-Corner

DRAPER'S BLUFF

Draper's Bluff sports the Southern Illinois area's tallest, high quality stone, measuring around 100-120 feet tall and over 2 miles long. Standing at the top of a forested ridge and visible from several miles away, the bluff's 2-pitch routes afford excellent training for multi-pitch climbing. Routes vary in type from the traditional of yesteryear to sport routes. The cliff is said to be a fine example of a Pennsylvanian escarpment, primarily sandstone with some limestone. It features slab, roofs, and everything in between. A pleasant warm-up hike from Cedar Grove Church takes about 15-20 minutes.

In the summer, the ticks during the approach give reason to make October through May the ideal months to climb at Draper's Bluff. On winter days with a biting north wind, Draper's south-face provides protection from the wind and it radiates the sun's heat. If it's 30 degrees in Carbondale, it can easily be 40-45 degrees on the rock. T-shirts in January have not been uncommon.

The Illinois Department of Natural Resources has acquired possession of Draper's Bluff, that being the southwest face left of *Bloody Nose* (Route #47). It is now part of Ferne Clyffe State Park. Check with Ferne Clyffe about the status of primitive camping prior to pitching your tent at that portion of the bluff. Also, be aware that the south, east, and north faces of Draper's Bluff are on private land. Therefore, you are on private land during the entire approach. **DO NOT GO TO DRAPER'S DURING DEER HUNTING SEASON**. Not only is it dangerous, it is also extremely aggravating to the hunters who had been looking forward to plugging the deer you just spooked. For information on hunting seasons in Southern Illinois, call the Illinois Dept. of Natural Resources Region 5 Office at **618-435-8138**. Historically, there has never been any problem between landowners and climbers at Draper's. Let's keep it that way. Be friendly to all locals and leave the boom box in the car.

For primitive camping, an ideal spot is the camping ledge (see route map, page). Take note that it is on the privately owned section of the bluff. Access the camping ledge from the 3rd class gully on its east side; level ground, a fire ring and a roof above are its only provisions. Don't be alarmed if you occasionally hear strange noises like an alien caught in a bear trap emanating from the farm near the road below. The hogs and cows periodically release the most heinous sounding groans.

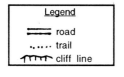

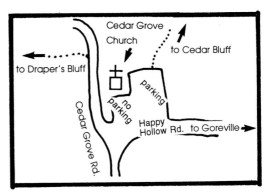

The Approach

See Cedar Bluff for the car approach & amenities (page 46). From the parking lot, hike past the church on Cedar Grove Road (west side of church) for 700 feet. Right before the hill, spot the last cedar tree on your left. The trail, marked by two posts, starts just past the tree on the left in a meadow. Cross the meadow, take a hard left and jump the stream. The path continues uphill and in between two shacks, skirting next to the shack on your right. The trail then enters the woods, crosses a wash, and eventually forks near the bottom of the bluff.

to Draper's Bluff

Northeast Face- Turn rightward at the fork and follow the bottom of the bluff line. You'll come to a large, 45 foot roof (the Loony Bin) that offers good pro from the rain. The routes below are in this area, listed <u>left to right</u>. Please don't disturb the local's fixed campsite!

1. **THE BATTLE WITHIN** 5.10c
It's the high angle slab sport route just left of the Loony Bin Roof. 4 QD + anchor.

2. **YABADABADEW** 5.13a
It's the headwall under the roof. Lieback the crack up and left to a small ledge 15 feet off the ground. Take the crystalline crack further until you can traverse 6 feet to the right through large pockets. From there, top out straight to the fixed belay.

3. **MADNESS VARIATION** 5.9
Begin 12 feet left of *High Anxiety* (#4). Ascend the face to the rightward lieback to start and climb into *High Anxiety*.
<u>Mixed pro</u>- varied sizes, 2 QD.

4. **HIGH ANXIETY** 5.9
At the right end of the Loony Bin Roof, start at the 10-foot high shelf. Ascend the leftward lieback crack for 8 feet. Step left and go up the broken, off-width lieback to the ledge. Traverse rightward. No anchor at present. The 1st ascent team bailed from a jammed sling.
Mixed pro- varied sizes, 2 QD

South Face- Turn left at the fork. Follow the trail around towards the south face. At the next intersection, take a hard left to follow the bottom of the bluff. Or, follow the rightward trail up the hill to go to the top . It will eventually run into the top trail that runs the length of the bluff. Head left (west) on the top trail. If you rappel to the ground, you'll need TWO ROPES as the average height of Draper's Bluff is 110 feet. A few of the 2-pitch routes have a midpoint anchor allowing two one-rope rappels. Some routes with top anchors are equipped with name identification which should aid you in getting about. In this guide for Draper's Bluff, routes indicated with "(rap in)" after the number grade should be approached from above. Take a mental note of the land's particulars if you like to climb until dark. Much thrashing about has occurred through the weeds & stickers. The beggar lice (I call it velcro weed) takes forever to remove from your clothing. Routes on the south & southwest faces are listed right to left.

1. **THE OVERHANG** 5.9
Located at the first large outcropping on the south face, the climb consists of a 15-foot face topped by a 3-foot roof on the right (east) end. Climb the thin crack through the overhang.

Continue westward to a large, boulder strewn, 2nd class gully- the easiest way to the top for over a half-mile. To the left of the gully is a buttress formation with a roof standing out from the bluff. On the inside face is a nice crack, *L2*.

2. **L2** 5.7+
Follow the lie-back crack up and rightward, around the corner (right) and up the delicate face. Fun lead. Natural pro- mid sizes

3. **L1** 5.4
It's the chimney between the buttress of Route #2 and the face. Climb to the large ledge under the overhang and walk off to the right.

4. **RODEO** 5.8/A2 or 5.12

Walk half-way up the aforementioned 2nd class gully and head left. Go across the ledge (atop Routes #2 & 3) under the roof. It's the 2-inch crack going up through the overhang. Begin where it's aidable or free the whole thing.
Natural pro- varied sizes
FA- Adam Grosowsky (in a cowboy hat), Alan Carrier '76

5. **WIRE BRUSH** 5.10

About 30 feet left of *L2* (#2), ascend the fingery, face crack that ends 10 feet below a large ledge. From the top of the crack exit left or right.

60 feet further left (west) of Route #5 is a chimney/gully marking the edge of the ledge.

6. **NO THANKS** 5.8

It's the small, squeeze chimney in the upper left part of the aforementioned chimney/gully. Either scramble up to it or traverse the ledge from the right.

7. **DEER CHASE** 5.9

About 25 feet left of the base of the big chimney, ascend a series of diagonal cracks, rightward up the wall. Follow the crack around the bottom overhang, go up and traverse right into the exit chimney.
Natural pro- varied sizes

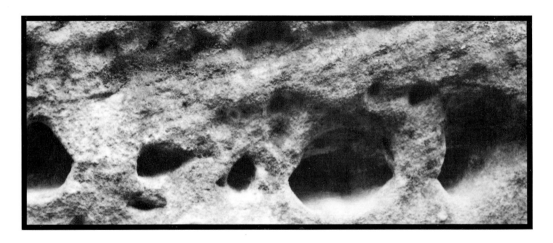

Follow the trail westward to a fence.

8. HIGH OVER CAMP 5.9+

A fence is located 50 feet right (east) of the route's base. Climb the crack starting left of a 15-foot high prow. The crack system offers easy ground to the exposed overhung section, scene of many a whipper. Craig Barnes and Gene Charleton did the FA with aid, giving it a 5.7/A3 rating. Alan Carrier nabbed the first free ascent on TR, giving it a very modest 5.9+ rating.
<u>Natural pro</u>- varied sizes

9. CHIMNEY 5.5

It's about 40 feet further west from Route #8 and just right of *The World's Saddest Dog* (#12). Ascend the obvious right-facing dihedral that forms a chimney.

10. MONROE'S MADNESS 5.4

Ascend *Chimney* (#9) for 30 feet, then traverse right onto the face and go up an easy lieback.

11. NASHVILLE SKYLINE 5.7

Do *Monroe's Madness* (#10), except skip the easy lieback and go about 20 feet further right. Ascend the tricky face.

12. WORLD'S SADDEST DOG 5.12a/b (rap in)

Take one of the 1st turn-ins off the top trail. It leads to a large, stone clearing by the edge. From there, the anchor should be about 25 feet left on top of the rounded corner. About 40 feet right (west), you'll also see the top anchors for Routes #16 & 17. Rap down and swing in to the belay shelf, which from the bottom, is also located 25 feet straight left of *Chimney* (#9). Bring 7 QD & a small stopper.
FA- Kerby McGhee, Andy Boone '91 Kerby was bummin' after seeing his dog get run over.

13. **BLACK WIDOW** 5.8

From *Chimney* (#9), walk about 60 feet down a slope to a small, inside corner (right-facing dihedral). Ascend this for about 20 feet into the base of a chimney/gully. Go rightward on the ledge to the base of *Chimney* route or ascend to the ledge at the base of *Burning Puppies* (#16) and *Cornbread* (#17) for a 2nd pitch. Natural pro- varied sizes

14. **BOOKSHELF BLUE** 5.9+/A1

About 100 feet left of *Black Widow* (#13), locate the face with a finger-to-hands crack that starts 15 feet off the ground. Pitch 1- Place pro from a shoulder stand or stick. Aid until freeable. Follow the crack up and left. Pass by the 2-bolt *(Blue Roof)* belay, go to the cedar tree & belay from there. Descend as with Route #15 or... Pitch 2- Scary squeeze above the belay through the chimney crack. The chimney crack defines the right side of the Rubik's Cube (the Cube is obvious from the road, see cliff map). Top out through slab/gully. Natural pro- varied sizes

15. **BLUE ROOF** 5.10/A1 (see cover)

Pitch 1- same as pitch 1 on Route #14, except stop at the fixed belay. Pitch 2- Traverse rightward beneath the large roof until you're standing on a plate-sized iron flake. Crank the obvious dihedral/roof crack. Natural pro- varied sizes, bring TCU's! Descent- rap anchor way right on shelf. **variation** (free start for 1st pitch) 5.12a/b- From the ground, start about 10 feet left & take the rib system that arches into the route.

14 15

From the ground, you can access *Burning Puppies & Cornbread* from *Black Widow* (#13).

16. **BURNING PUPPIES** 5.10b (rap in)
See *World's Saddest Dog* (#12) for top approach. Step down a 4 foot ledge to access the anchor. It's a slab sport route on the west side of a large gully. Rap to a grassy ledge at the base of the route. 5 QD + anchor.

17. **CORNBREAD** 5.11a (rap in)
The anchor lies 5 feet west of the *Burning Puppies* (#16) anchor. 5 QD + anchor.

18. **INBRED HOOLIGANS** 5.11a TR
From the top of *Cornbread* (#17), look 50 feet westward to the perpendicular face. The route goes up the middle to the obvious cedar tree. Access the tree via the *Hein Dog* (#19) approach.

Blue Roof

19. **HEIN DOG** 5.13a (rap in)
It's the right, face route up the center of the Rubik's Cube. From the top, it's the next protruding section of the cliff, west of *Burning Puppies* (#16). The second turn-in off the top trail should take you to the anchor for *Hein Dog* and *Kittens*. It's right below a small cedar tree on a shelf near the edge. Rap about half-way down the cliff to a fixed anchor on a sloping shelf. Begin 10 feet right (east) & go straight up, paralleling the 2nd pitch of *Kittens*. 5 QD + anchor.

20. **KITTENS** 5.12b & 5.11b (same top anchor as *Hein Dog* #19)
Walking underneath the Rubik's Cube left of *Blue Roof* (#15), it's the sport route starting out with eye-bolts. Pitch 1- Head up the face below the Rubik's Cube. Includes a short rightward traverse. Belay at the fixed anchor on a sloping shelf. Pitch 2 (5.11b)- It's the left face route up the center of the Rubik's Cube. Pull over a small, overhanging dihedral above the belay onto the upper wall and follow the line. Bring several QD. A small Friend at the top of Pitch 2 might help you relax a bit during the exit moves.

Eric Ulner riding on *Rodeo*, Draper's Bluff

Jim Thurmond on his classic, *The Outline*, Draper's Bluff

21. SUNDAY PICNIC 5.7

Pitch 1- Just left of the start of *Kittens* (#20), go up the flaring crack into the chimney. Belay at the big ledge. Pitch 2- Continue in the same crack to the top (crack defines the left side of the Rubik's Cube).
Natural pro- big stuff

22. THE WITCH OF THE UPPER MEADOW 5.12a (rap in)

Take the top trail turn-in toward the anchor for Route #19. Just prior to the stone clearing, head about 75 feet rightward (west). The anchor is located along the most narrow strip of exposed stone between the edge and the grass. Rappel about 50 feet to a big ledge and begin. From the bottom of the cliff, the route is leftward (west) of *Sunday Picnic* (#21) belay ledge on the upper wall.
Mixed pro- 2 QD, set of TCU's, + anchor.

23. THRUTCH 5.8/A1

Ascend the huge chimney about 60 feet left of *Sunday Picnic* (#21). It's just right of *The Outline* (#24). Aid around a bulge to access it, using the thin crack 10 feet left.
Natural pro- varied sizes

24. THE OUTLINE 5.12a

It's starts about 20 feet left of *Thrutch* (#23). Pitch 1- Tricky moves take you to a juggy iron flake at the 1st clip. Follow the broken crack system to the anchor. Pitch 2- Pull the roof & go straight up the face.

25. OUTLINE VARIATION 5.12a

at the 3rd clip, cut left to *Smell the Coffee* (#26).

Routes #26 & #27 are easily identified for their obvious difficulty, length, & eye-bolts.

26. SMELL THE COFFEE 5.13a/b

It's just left of Route #24. Climb to the ledge. Right top-out version is *Bavarian Chocolate* 5.12a. Left top-out version is *Hazelnut* 5.12a/b. 20 QD + anchor.

27. **SON OF A PREACHERMAN** 5.13a/b

It's just left of Route #26. Up to the shelf is 5.12a. Harder stuff's up the 'hang. 20 QD + anchor.

28. **DIRECT EXPOSURE** 5.11b (alternate 1st pitch for Route #29)

About 65 feet off the ground & just left of Route #27, locate the protruding ledge with an iron plate/flake at its lip. This route comes up the line below it. A slab with 1 safety-bolt takes you to a small, left-facing dihedral with a so-so fixed pin. Go straight up to a small shelf, then traverse outward onto the right side of the protruding ledge to a fixed belay. See route #29 for 2nd pitch info. Mixed pro- 2 QD, varied sizes (#4 Camalot) + anchor

29. **SOUTHERN EXPOSURE** 5.10a

Start 20 feet left of Route #28. Pitch 1- Go straight up on good flakes to the first roof. Traverse rightward in the horizontal crack system under the roof and pass beneath the iron plate/flake. Go straight up to a small shelf, then traverse outward onto the right side of the protruding ledge to a fixed belay- a great squat. Natural pro- varied sizes. Pitch 2 (5.9+)- From the belay, traverse about 20 feet left to a gully/break in the roof- casual spot to fish for a big piece. Go up and slightly right to the line of fixed pro. It is southern exposure!
Mixed pro- 3 QD, big Hex, + anchor
FA- Alan Carrier, Steve Mestdagh '79 Alan led the 2nd pitch on-sight with no fixed pro.
"Hmm...no words coming from Alan...I haven't heard a 'biner click, yet I've fed 40 feet of rope", thought Steve as he looked again at his belay anchor.

Back on the ground below *Southern Exposure* (#29), continue westward down the slope & around the corner to a 3rd class gully. It accesses the roof protected Camping Ledge. The Camping Ledge averages about 20 feet wide, 100 yards long and 40 feet in height.

30. MIKE'S CLIMB 5.8
Walking about 45 feet left (west) of the 3rd class gully, locate the 45-50 foot wide alcove with opposing cracks. Ascend the left-facing dihedral/crack on the right to the ledge.
Natural pro- varied sizes

31. PUPPET MASTER 5.9
45 feet to the left of *Mike's Climb* (#30), ascend the crack to the ledge.
Natural pro- varied sizes

32. SAMANTHA 5.13a
It's around the corner and down the sloped path about 140 feet left (west) of *Puppet Master* (#31). It starts in a fairly thin and overhung, natural pro crack. Traverse rightward at the top of the crack. Fixed pro takes you through the crux to the Camping Ledge.
Mixed pro- small stuff for the crack, 3 QD for the crux up high.

33. BAD DAY 5.7
About 75 feet left (west) of *Samantha,* locate the leftward leaning, left-facing dihedral/crack behind a big boulder. It marks the west end of the Camping Ledge. Ascend the crack for 10 feet, traverse left onto the face and top out on the ledge.
<u>Natural pro</u>- big stuff

34. NO NAME 2 5.8
A bit to right of *No Name 1* (#35) and still on the Camping Ledge, it's the short, diagonal lead up the steep wall.
<u>Natural pro</u>- varied sizes

35. NO NAME 1 5.7
2nd pitch above the Camping Ledge. From the top of *Bad Day* (#33), walk rightward (east) on the ledge to a slight yield in the overhang, where it appears to be scooped out. Gary Monroe & Craig Barnes did the FA on aid (A2), then Mike Azrin freed it at 5.8. <u>Natural pro</u>- varied sizes

36. TRIAL AND ERROR 5.7/A3 or 5.11
About 70 feet left (west) of *Bad Day* (#35), it's the obvious crack with a V-shaped flair. The crack overhangs at the bottom. One long pitch. According to Adam Grosowsky's *The Gritstone Mountaineer,* "...route had a history of failure, including some neat aid falls from under the roof."
<u>Natural pro</u>- varied sizes, old pin near the top

37. MICKEY MOUSE 5.4
About 100 feet up the slope, left of Route #36, it's the only 5.4 looking thing around, but it's sort of "vegetated". It goes about 60 feet.

38. THE LADY OR THE TIGER? 5.10a
About 35 feet left of Route #37, ascend the sport route. 7 QD + anchor

Bill Rogers on *Ant Killer*

39. **ANT KILLER** 5.9
Truly one of the classic trad routes of the Midwest. About 30 feet left (west) of Route #38, it's
the obvious, right-facing dihedral that goes 75 feet to a ledge. Nasty fall if you blow the exit
move onto the ledge. From the ledge, either rap from the fixed anchor or do the 2nd pitch. <u>Pitch
2</u>- If you're up for it- Ascend the 5.6 crack with the tree in the way and traverse left into the exit
chimney. <u>Natural pro</u>- small-mid size stoppers all the way up Pitch 1. The keen eye may notice
the iron plate/flake near the top of the 1st pitch. A 9/16" sling may remove the "nasty" potential.
Variation 5.9+ Ascend the thin crack to the right. Where it ends, traverse leftward to *Ant Killer*
and go up. <u>Natural pro</u>- small wires, square nuts

40. **"C"** 5.7

It's the obvious crack just around the corner, 60 feet left (west) of *Ant Killer* (#39). Ascend the crack to the base of the overhang and traverse rightward to the fixed anchor on the *Ant Killer* belay ledge. A very popular lead.

Natural pro- varied sizes

Direct variation (5.8)- Don't traverse at the top. Stay with the overhang-crack.

41. **TRAVERSE ROUTE** 5.9

From the top of *"C"*, traverse rightward across the *Ant Killer* (#39) belay ledge and continue all the way to the top of *Bad Day* (#33) at The Camping Ledge. Take the line of least resistance. It's about 4 or 5 pitches across. Natural pro- varied sizes

42. **ROLL-AIDS** 5.6/A3 or 5.9

About 25 feet left of the start of *"C"* (#40), ascend the rising crack under a flake that meets *"C"* under the overhang.

Natural pro- varied sizes

43. INDIGESTION 5.9

About 20 feet left of *Roll-Aids* (#42), take the big crack up to base of the overhang. Traverse rightward to the top of *"C"* (#40). A rotten, sandy route.
<u>Natural pro</u>- varied sizes

44. SCHEACHER'S DEMISE 5.9

About 35 feet left (west) of *Indigestion* (#43), locate the 5.7 looking crack. Ascend the crack until it ends about 40 feet up. Traverse left to finish.
<u>Natural pro</u>- varied sizes

The trail steepens after *Scheacher's Demise* (#44) & bends around a corner. About 50 feet further left (west) is a tomato-shape boulder known as Tomato Rock. Tomato Rock boulder makes up the upper two-thirds of this section of the bluff.

45. SUNSHINE FACE 5.9+

It's located to the right of Tomato Rock. Ascend the middle of the low-angle face. Take the line of least resistance. Ascend the right-facing dihedral crack to the top. Usually done in 2 pitches to avoid drag.
<u>Natural pro</u>- varied sizes

46. NO NAME 5.12 TR

In the middle of Tomato Rock, climb the face and go straight up and out the prominent roof.

47. TOMATO TURNPIKE 5.7/A2 or 5.9

It's the big crack at the left edge of Tomato Rock.
<u>Natural pro</u>- varied sizes

The next 4 routes listed are located at what is known as the A-Corner. Past the A-Corner begins the southwest face of Draper's, which has become property of Ferne Clyffe State Park.

48. BLOODY NOSE 5.6

Pitch 1- About 40 feet down the slope (west) from Tomato Rock, ascend the chimney/dihedral to a shelf. Belay near the obvious tree. Careful! It's gotten very creaky. Pitch 2- traverse way out left, around the corner. Belay by the small cedar tree growing out of the rock to avoid drag, then top out through the crack above it. Natural pro- varied sizes. A favorite of Jim Logue's, local climber from Springfield, Illinois. He was a Supervisor of Vehicles for the US Postal Service. Jim died in 1991 following a spirited battle with cancer. Route dedicated by friends.
variation (5.8)- Traverse rightward from the belay shelf for the 2nd pitch.

49. NEVER PASS A CHANCE TO GET PUMPED... 5.10+ About 30 feet down the slope
(west) from *Bloody Nose* (#48), locate the prominent hand/finger crack. Pitch 1 (5.10+)-
Ascend the crack until it ends, and continue up the face to a fixed anchor on a round ledge beneath the bulge/roof. Steve Mestdagh originally gunned it on-sight from the crack to the roof with no fixed pro. Sick, sick!
Mixed pro- small-mid sizes, 1 QD + anchor.
FA- Steve Mestdagh, Sean Scuras, Linda Schneider 1981

50. ...JETSETTER 5.12d (5.11d variation)

Pitch 2 Route #49- *(Never Pass a Chance)*- Go out the roof and up the face. 5 QD + anchor.
Rappel approach- hike the top trail to the A-Corner where the cliff turns to face southwest. The top anchor is out on the corner.
variation (5.11d)- Pull the roof, then traverse leftward to easier climbing on the arete.

About 20 feet downhill and around the corner (northwest) from *Jetsetter* (#50), step away from the cliff and hop onto the boulder. Looking up at the wall, locate the fixed anchor part-way up the face for *She's Diggin' My Scene,* route #51.

51. SHE'S DIGGIN' MY SCENE 5.6
Sketchy natural pro all the way to the anchor.

52. NORM REED'S CLIMB 5.12c/d TR
Ascend Route #51. Then go up & left through the middle of the short roof above. Skirt right and go up to the ledge.

53. THIN MAN 5.5
About 20 feet left of Route #52, ascend the obvious chimney/gully.

54. HE MAN'S BIG ADVENTURE 5.9
About 10 feet left of *Thin Man* (#53), start at the bulging face at the bottom. Go up to where the face meets a decent crack. Take it up to a ledge. Exit to *Thin Man.*

Over 200 feet to the left of the A-Corner, locate the 15 foot high overhang known as The Cattle Cave.

55. TINY DANCER 5.9/A1
The route starts near a big tree at an obvious, thin crack beginning at the lip of the Cattle Cave overhang. Once on the large ledge, exit rightward beneath the overhang to the chimney.
Natural pro- varied sizes.

56. FLYING SQUIRREL 5.11
It's the next crack route, about 30 feet left of *Tiny Dancer* (#55) & at the left end of the Cattle Cave. Pitch 1 (5.11)- Crank the roof-crack moves to start. Ascend the crack to the trees and belay. Pitch 2 (5.7)- Take the exit gully to the left.
Natural pro- varied sizes.

57. F--K'N "A" RIGHT PECKERHEAD 5.11a/5.9
It's located about 20 feet left of *Flying Squirrel* (#56). <u>Pitch 1</u>- Start on the bulge below the prominent, thin horns 25 feet up the route. Climb straight up and belay under the roof at the top. <u>Pitch 2</u>- (5.9)- Traverse 35 feet leftward to a protectable break in the upper roof. Top out straight above. <u>Natural pro</u>- varied sizes.

About 40 feet to the left of *Peckerhead* (#57) is a 3rd class gully that accesses the top.

58. LOST HIGHWAY 5.9+
Standing at the bottom of the 3rd class gully, locate the large chimney up and right. The route follows the left-facing dihedral crack system. <u>Pitch 1</u>- Start on the crack 5 feet to the right of the base of the chimney. Climb it to the shelf beneath a large roof and belay. <u>Pitch 2</u>- Traverse rightward until you're beneath an ironing-board shaped roof. Ascend through the notch on the left. Follow the face straight up. Exit slightly rightward.
<u>Natural pro</u>- varied sizes

59. GENUINE RISK 5.11
Over 100 feet to the left (northwest) of the 3rd class gully and around a sharp corner, locate a large fallen tree. The route starts in the corner, in front of the tree's base. Two separate cracks, beginning 10 feet apart, meet a roof 20 feet off the ground. Ascend the left crack going out of the roof, follow it to a bulge at the top, then exit rightward.
Natural pro- varied sizes.

Just past *Genuine Risk* (#59) is a fence.

60. TUMBLING DICE 5.10
About 300 feet past the fence, locate a broken crack system capped by a 6-foot roof. A large chimney is 25 feet to the left. Ascend the face crack, following it as it angles slightly left. Traverse left on brittle rock (hence the name) beneath the roof to a cedar tree in the aforementioned chimney. Belay at the tree, then rappel from it to exit.
Natural pro- varied sizes through #4 Friend

FERNE CLYFFE STATE PARK

Jim Schneider on *First Born*

Ferne Clyffe State Park is home to many a fine TR, high quality bouldering, a few fine natural leads, & an occasional winter ice climb (see page 2 for *Shades of Gray*).. Although the Park's management has in recent years placed high restrictions on where one may climb, the section that is allowed is worth a visit. As with Giant City, you have easy approaches, paved roads, & ample parking.

Not to digress, but I do wonder sometimes about the rationale used for closing climbing areas around America. If it's, "Humans & heights don't mix. People have been falling off here & we just can't let it happen anymore", then why aren't our lakes being closed as well? Humans & water mix about as well. People drown every year, but that doesn't cause near the media commotion as someone falling from a cliff. Anyway, where were we?

Amenities

Campsites, showers, telephones, water, & electricity are all available in the Park. For other options, see Cedar Bluff on page 46.

The Approach

The Park is located just south of Goreville off of Highway 37. Signs guide you from all directions. When you enter the park, go left at the 1st stop sign toward the picnic areas. At the next fork, turn right and follow the road to the end and park. Cross the stream with the artificial stepping stones on the north side of the end parking lot. Follow the mowed grass trail to the main, west-facing bluff ahead and to the right. A sign in front of the bluff marks it as the only cliff in the park that is presently open for climbing. Routes #10-14 are easily visible from the sign. Routes are listed right to left, and all of them are TR unless lead gear is listed.

Cindy Hart bouldering on Pump Wall (area now closed)

The first 4 routes listed begin at "Three Humps Corner" (see cliff map). The humps are divided apart by 4 slabby cracks, Routes 1-4

1. **NO HANS SOLO**
It's the far right gully/crack. Tricky no hands route (been soloed).
FA- Darth Vader

2. **TEETERING TICK FEST** 5.8
It's the 2nd gully/crack from the right, about 30 feet left of Route #1.

3. **FIRST CLIMB** (aka *psychopath*) 5.2
The 3rd gully/crack from the right, it's about 25 feet left of Route #2. A horizontal tree is on top.

4. **QUASIMODO** 5.6
It's about 20 feet left of Route #3. Stay left of the Evergreen tree up above. Crank the overhang on top too!

5. **DITCH PITCH** 5.4
It's the obvious chimney climb to the left of Route #4.

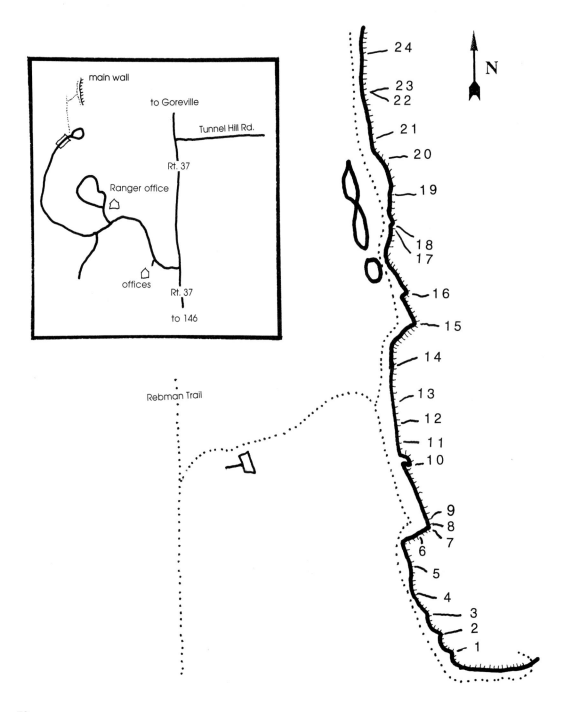

main wall

to Goreville

Tunnel Hill Rd.

Rt. 37

Ranger office

offices

Rt. 37

to 146

Rebman Trail

N

24
23
22
21
20
19
18
17
16
15
14
13
12
11
10
9
8
7
6
5
4
3
2
1

Continuing around the corner, about 25 feet left of Route #5...

6. TWO TIMES TOUGH 5.7
It's the center of the short section of face to the left of the corner.

7. I DON'T CARE (aka *Open Book*) 5.4
It's the 90 degree dihedral/crack just left of Route #6.

8. JENNIFER GOES TO HOLLYWOOD 5.11a
Climb the face just left of Route #7, avoiding the crack.

9. PONDERING PERPETUAL MOTION 5.11c/d
Start 6 feet left of *Jennifer Goes...* Go up & slightly left.

10. HAWK'S BEAK 5.7
Toward the right end of the bluff (as you face it), it's the obvious chimney with a finger-crack in the back of it. A 10-foot high dihedral roof marks the bottom of the route.
Natural pro- varied sizes, excellent stances.

11. MISSOURI BREAKS 5.9+ TR
About 30 feet left of *Hawk's Beak,* an overhanging start on big holds takes you to a thin and fairly continuous vertical crack that angles slightly rightward.

12. GOREVILLE EATING SOCIETY 5.10c
It's about 20 feet left of Route #11. Go up through the big pockets, angling slightly leftward. Continue straight through the shallow gully/wash & on through the overhung top-out.

13. RUSTY PIN 5.6 A1 or 5.10
About 30 feet left of Route #11, the route starts in the hand crack at the lip of the low roof. Follow the large, snaking crack to the top. Aid or free the start.
Natural pro- varied sizes

14. NO HOLDS BARRED 5.12a
About 35 feet left of Route #13, follow the crack half way up. Traverse 20 feet rightward along the sloping shelf. Pull the overhang & go straight up.

Continue 25 feet left to the blunt corner...

15. UNDER THE INFLUENCE 5.8
It's the 1st dihedral crack, left of the blunt corner & inside the woods.
Natural pro- varied sizes

16. GEORGE OF THE JUNGLE 5.11d
About 40 feet left of Route #15 is an overhung dihedral with an arete to its right. Start just left of the arete. Go up the overhang, following the arete to the top. Potential pendulum for- "George, George, George of the jungle- watch out for that...!"

17. FIRST BORN 5.10a
About 80 feet left of Route #15, start at the base of the overhung, rightward angling arete. Go straight up the face, staying out of the dihedral.

18. MILES FROM NOWHERE 5.7
It starts 6 feet left of Route #16. It's a pretty obvious dihedral/crack.

Continuing left of Route #17, walk 40 feet through a hallway formed by boulders on your left. At the end of the first boulder, look up to the right on the main wall to a thin, finger flake.

19. DIVINE INTERVENTION 5.10a
Take the thin finger flake until you're standing atop the narrow, foot-and-a-half shelf. Top out straight above.

20. CRACKED HEART 5.7
It's the hand-sized crack 18 feet left of Route #18
Natural Pro- varied sizes

Layla (tied in) & Jessie Davidson on Girlfriend Rock, Opie's Kitchen

Nighttime Tyrolean traverse into a Trillium forest. Dr. Robert Haugh of Team Columbia Sportswear, training for the Eco-Challenge endurance race.

The Short Wall

The Short Wall starts about 20 feet left of Route #19. It's a fairly smooth, high angle slab averaging about 25 feet tall.

21. MR. MO JO RISING 5.12A
Starts at the right side of The Short Wall. Go straight up the face toward a cedar tree. Route named for Sam, a Ferne Clyffe Park Ranger.

The following 3 routes are dedicated to Southern Illinois climber, Margy Roth, who died in August of '95 following a long battle with cancer.

22. GRACE UNDER FIRE 5.11c
Locate two plate-sized iron flakes about 5 feet off the ground in the center of The Short Wall. It begins just right of the right flake & goes up & slightly rightward at the top. Got it right?

23. THE GIFT 5.10c
Start at Route #21 & go straight up.

24. CHILLY, GRAY MATTER 5.11
About 10 left of Route #22, go through the short & thin, vertical seam.

JACKSON FALLS

Jackson Falls makes up the southeastern portion of the Jackson Hollow area (named after Jackson Orange, who once owned the land). The heavily forested hollow is surrounded by pocketed sandstone cliffs, some reaching over 70 feet in height. Several free-standing towers enhance the canyon's mystique with their route-filled hallways. In the winter and spring seasons (primarily), the south-southwest flowing creek feeds the north waterfall. Sunny days in late spring are ideal for swimming in the 12+ foot-deep pool. A very large turtle lives in it, so you may want to keep your pants on, guys. When the pool stagnates in the summer, you can still find relief in the spring-fed, albeit shallow section of the creek in the center of the canyon.

Out of all the local areas, Jackson Falls has the highest concentration of routes. In the late 70's, TR's and natural leads were being opened on the west side of the railroad tracks, although parties would occasionally wander over to climb near the R.R. Rock area. Since 1985, the push has been to open routes on the east side of the tracks especially since the Forest Service does not want climbers to climb on the west side of the tracks. They view the east side more suitable for recreational use. Since natural lines have been climbed out, the emphasis has been on opening sport routes, and mixed routes whenever the pro is decent. Mixed routes usually call for both wedging and (more often) camming pro. Incredibly hard to flash routes are abundant. In fact, the most common grade is 5.12. Potential 5.14's hang throughout the canyon- their very existence denying any need for alteration.

Camping at Jackson Falls is free, but primitive. Well, not completely primitive- you can camp out of your car. **If you're determined to camp below the cliffs in the hollow, please do not pitch your tent on the trail or near the main pool.** There's really not much point in camping by the pool, as you can get an equivalent "wilderness" experience next to your car. Tents in the trail force foot traffic off the trail. Not good. Also, refrain from creating new camp fire rings. There seem to be plenty already. The Forest Service does not come in and clean or maintain the area. It shouldn't even have to be stated, but I will anyway- All climbers should feel equally responsible to tend climbing areas. Everyone owns public lands together, right?

Amenities

The closest U.S. Forest Service campground to Jackson Falls is at Bell Smith Springs. Road signs will guide your way. For a few bucks a night, you'll get a level campsite with a picnic table and grill, water, and vault toilets. For a U.S.F.S. campground with showers and a beach, head to Lake Glendale Recreational Area (see Jackson Falls road map). Marion (40 minutes from Jackson) and Carbondale (1 hour) have the largest concentration of motels/hotels and restaurants.

The Approach

From Highway 45, head east on Ozark Road. Another 4 1/2 miles will land you at an intersection marked by Zion Church and Cemetery. Hang a left, go about 2 hundred yards to the 1st farmhouse and turn right. A mile or so further, you'll be easing your car down the steep hill toward the creek. The main parking area is on the right at the bottom of the hill.

If you've been around for the past few years, you'll fondly remember the muffler-eating entrance hill & parking lot. Thanks to a road maintenance swap between the Forest Service & Pope County, nice improvements (hopefully permanent) have been made to the entrance hill.

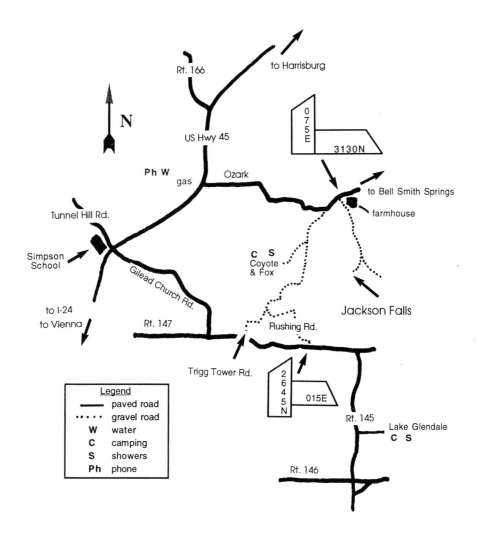

The squeaky gear... If the hill should erode again, however, and you're forced to park above the hill, make sure to allow room for others to pass (duh) and **DO NOT PARK IN THE DRIVE-WAY** of the obvious barn and farmhouse. Also, do not camp anywhere above the hill. The local landowners will not appreciate your presence.

A 2-minute walk from the parking area will take you to the ladder-tree next to the main waterfall. Beware that both the ladder & its support tree could & eventually will fail. During the summer of '95, one of the tree's main branches broke. So, switch modes before you head down it on autopilot for your hundredth time. The closest alternative canyon entry is the dog-walk gully near the east falls (see J. Falls overview map).

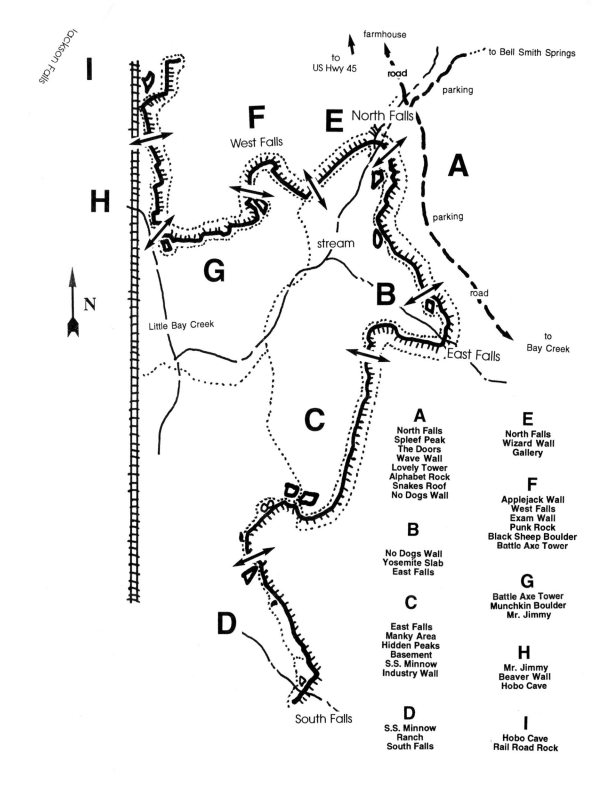

Jackson Falls

I

to US Hwy 45

to
farmhouse

road

to Bell Smith Springs

parking

F
West Falls

E

North Falls

A

H

stream

parking

G

road

B

Little Bay Creek

East Falls

to
Bay Creek

N

C

D

South Falls

A
North Falls
Spleef Peak
The Doors
Wave Wall
Lovely Tower
Alphabet Rock
Snakes Roof
No Dogs Wall

B
No Dogs Wall
Yosemite Slab
East Falls

C
East Falls
Manky Area
Hidden Peaks
Basement
S.S. Minnow
Industry Wall

D
S.S. Minnow
Ranch
South Falls

E
North Falls
Wizard Wall
Gallery

F
Applejack Wall
West Falls
Exam Wall
Punk Rock
Black Sheep Boulder
Battle Axe Tower

G
Battle Axe Tower
Munchkin Boulder
Mr. Jimmy

H
Mr. Jimmy
Beaver Wall
Hobo Cave

I
Hobo Cave
Rail Road Rock

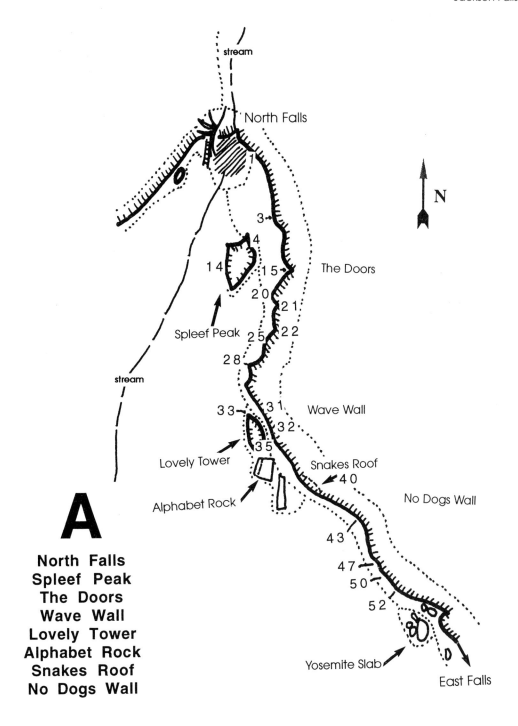

N

stream

North Falls

1

3→

4

14   15→

The Doors

20

21

Spleef Peak   25   22

28

33   31   Wave Wall

32

35

Lovely Tower   Snakes Roof

40

Alphabet Rock   No Dogs Wall

43

47

50

52

Yosemite Slab

East Falls

A

North Falls
Spleef Peak
The Doors
Wave Wall
Lovely Tower
Alphabet Rock
Snakes Roof
No Dogs Wall

North Falls Area

Routes to the right (as you're facing the cliff wall) or east of the main pool...

1. **HYDRA** 5.12c
It's the 1st route to the right of the pool. 3 QD + anchor.

2. **PUFF** 5.11a
Just right of *Hydra* (#1). 2 QD + anchor.

3. **THE BOW** 5.9 TR
It's the slanted dihedral lieback about 70 feet right of *Puff* (#2). Low quality.

Spleef Peak

Spleef Peak is the 1st free-standing tower to the east of the North Falls.

4. <u>**STORM WATCH**</u> 5.12b
Mono's start you out. 3 QD + anchor.

5. <u>**HEAVY HORSES**</u> 5.12b
Very fingery start off a menacing boulder. 3 QD + anchor.

6. **SONGS FROM THE WOOD** 5.10a/b
Funky lieback start just left of Route #5.
<u>Mixed pro</u>- 3 QD, mid-size stopper, + anchor.

7. **DANCING ON THE JETTY** 5.9
Low traffic, stepped slab about 10 feet left of Route #6.
<u>Natural pro</u>- a set of TCU's.

8. **THE TIN** 5.10a TR
Start on the bouldery, triangular face and go straight up.

9. THE GARDEN ROUTE 5.10a
Goes up the right side of the high angle slab.
<u>Mixed pro</u>- 2 QD, TCU's for the middle +
anchor.
variation (5.7)- Go about half way up the
lieback 5 feet left. Top out on *Garden.*

10. THROUGH THE SMOKE 5.9 TR
A bit left of Route #9's variation, take the
crack all the way. Fixed anchor, common with
#11.

11. RATTLER 5.10a R
It's the next crack system, left of Route #10.
<u>Mixed pro</u>- 2 QD, mid-size stopper for the top,
+ anchor.

12. <u>MASTER MARLEY</u> 5.10a
A popular route- 3 move wonder.
Down at the left corner, start on the face and
move onto the arete. 3 QD + anchor.

13. CRACK TO INFINITY 5.12c TR
Around the corner from *Master Marley* (#12),
it's the 1st crack.

14. <u>LOVIN' THE RAIN</u> 5.12b
Wide solution crack left of Route #13. Exit rightward. 6 QD should do you fine.

David Hart on *Master Marley*

The Doors

The Doors is the area containing 3 prominent dihedrals, starting about 150 feet right (east) of the North Falls and facing Spleef Peak.

15. L.A. WOMAN 5.11
The 1st dihedral of The Doors nearest to Route #3. Lieback the crack to the good face holds on the right. Top out straight up. <u>Mixed pro</u>- varied sizes and 1 QD.
variation- I'm Your Back Door Man 5.11
Start on Route #16 & diagonal up & left on the face to *L.A. Woman.*

16. <u>LADIE'S CHOICE</u> 5.10
Off-width angling leftward into *L.A. Woman* (#15). <u>Natural pro</u>- mid-big sizes pretty decent pro

17. <u>ANGRY CHILD</u> 5.12b
Starts 15 feet right of *Ladie's Choice* (#16). 4 QD + anchor.

18. **CRO-MAGNON WARRIOR** 5.12b
Power lieback route in the middle of the wall. 5 QD + anchor.

19. **DIGITAL DELICATESSEN** 5.12a
Begins about 15 feet left of the right corner, *Amoeba Brains* (#20). Traverses rightward to top out on *Amoeba*. 4 QD + anchor on lip.

20. **AMOEBA BRAINS** 5.10c
It's the tricky arete where the trail meets the main wall coming from Spleef Peak. Often stick clipped. 3 QD + anchor on slab.

21. **KEEPERS OF THE SKILL** 5.11a
Located about 25 feet right of *Amoeba Brains* (#20), it's the 2nd dihedral of The Doors. Nice lieback crack.
Mixed pro- varied sizes and 2 QD.

22. **MORNING BEERS** 5.9 R
The 3rd dihedral of The Doors.
Natural pro- small-mid size. Committing lead.

23. **THE STAIN** 5.11d
Obvious black streak 5 feet right of *Morning Beers* (#22). 4 QD + anchor.

24. **THE TWIST** 5.11c
10' right of *The Stain* (#23). 3 QD + anchor.

25. **BROAD SWORD** 5.10b
It's the natural line about 15 feet right of *The Twist* (#24). Protects well.
Natural pro- varied sizes

26. **FANCY FEET** 5.11a
It's the sport route about 20 feet right of Route #25. Tops out through solution off-width. 4 QD + anchor.
variation (5.12a)- stay left of the 2nd safety-bolt & go straight up.

27. **BEASTIE** 5.11a
Just right of *Fancy Feet* (#26), go straight up the flaring off-width section. mid-size pro, 3 QD + anchor.

28. **DANCING BEAR** 5.12b
Continuing right, it's the route just prior to the overhang at the next corner. Blind bulges. Exit through the wash up and right or straight above. 4 QD + anchor. Bottom can protect naturally.

29. **CYBER SEX** 5.12b
Just right of #28, it starts at the 15 foot high left angling crack in the overhang. 4 QD + anchor.

30. **LITHUANIAN CHIMNEY** 5.8 TR
Continuing around the corner, it marks the right edge of the blank roof.

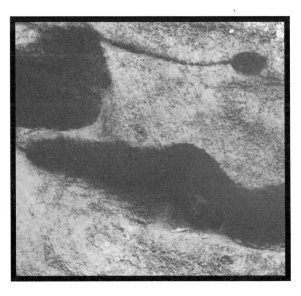

Wave Wall

The Wave Wall is the rippled face across the hallway from the Lovely Tower.

31. **PROJECT X** 5.12b TR
Super smearin' slab at the left end. Short, but extremely challenging. Go ahead- try it in August.

32. **FINE NINE** 5.9
Right end of Wave Wall. 4 QD + anchor.

Barb Knowles on *Lovely Arete*

Lovely Tower

33. <u>LOST INNOCENCE</u> 5.12c
Coming from the North Falls, it's the 1st route on the Lovely Tower prior to stepping into the hallway. 5 QD + anchor.

34. <u>HIDDEN TREASURE</u> 5.12a
Thin face route inside the hallway across from Route #32. 4 QD + anchor in tree.

35. <u>LOVELY ARETE</u> 5.11a
Blunt arete left of Route #34. 3 QD + anchor in tree.

36. <u>VELVET GREEN</u> 5.12a
Starts 10 feet left of *Lovely Arete* (#35). Traverses slightly right at first. 4 QD + anchor.

37. <u>RAIN DOG</u> 5.12b
Starts at the base of *Lefty Crack* (#38). Go straight up. 4 QD.

38. <u>LEFTY CRACK</u> 5.7 TR
It's the huge, leftward leaning crack on the Lovely Tower.

Alphabet Rock

   Kids' Climbing. Alphabet Rock is the large boulder just past Lovely Tower. It has a vertical wall opposite from Routes #36-38. Scamper up its side slab to access fixed TR anchors for great kids' routes. The back side has some pretty hard looking bouldering under an overhang.

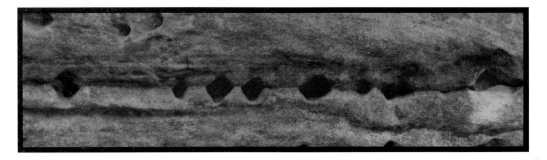

Snakes Roof Area

On the main wall, just past Lovely Tower & Alphabet Rock, you'll walk beneath the next obvious landmark, Snakes Roof. A quality bouldering traverse is underneath.

39. **THE BITCH** 5.12a TR
It's the small crack in a dihedral going out the left end of Snakes Roof.

40. <u>**HERE COME THE SNAKES**</u> 5.12c
Obvious sport route going out the middle of the roof. 3 QD + anchor.

41. **SHERMAN'S ROUTE** 5.11b TR
Start about 20 feet rightward, around the corner from Snakes Roof. Angle up and left. Done in the best of style, surely.
FA- Verm '89

42. **HUNTER'S ARROW** 5.10a
It's the 1st, large dihedral crack past (rightward) Snakes Roof. Great pro placing stances.
<u>Natural pro</u>- varied sizes. A big Friend at the top is nice to have.
FA- Jim Thurmond, Hunter Rafferty '87 I wonder who they named the route after?

43. **NO DOGS ALLOWED** 5.12b

It's the next sport route to the right of *Hunter's Arrow* (#42) Thin edges take you to big iron flakes. 5 QD, sling for last flake, + anchor. Thin face section originally hooked with a TR belay.

1st on-sight solo- Chris Ecklund '91 very respectable (ask Chris how his day ended)
direct variation- go straight up, skipping the 2nd clip and the edge next to it.

44. **DIRTY DIAPERS** A3

About 30 feet right of Route #43, follow the shallow crack in the right-facing dihedral up and across, beneath the overhang. Exit up and right.
FA- Mike Cremeens '92 Mike must have certainly packed his shorts when he fell on a "0" TCU.

45. **THE BEACH** 5.12b TR

Start 10 feet right of Route #44 on the iron flakes. Exit straight above through the slight break in the big overhang. The amount of loose sand qualified it.

46. **PUPPY POOP VARIATION** 5.9 TR

Start at the base of *The Beach* (#45). Take the *Dirty Diapers* (#44) exit.

47. **NO DANCERS** 5.11a/b

About 40 feet right of *The Beach* (#45), locate a 3-foot overhang about 15 feet high. This climb is at the left end of it. Climb the short face & pull the roof to the obvious crack
Mixed pro- 2 QD & a set of TCU's.

48. **BRASS** 5.11b TR

Just right of *No Dancers* (#47), ascend the middle of the short face & go straight over the roof. Exit leftward in the crack.

49. **EXPRESSIONS** 5.12a

It starts about 20 feet right of Route #48 & just left of *The Vow* (#50). 5 QD + anchor.

50. **THE VOW** 5.11c

It's the way obvious, 5.9 looking, open book gully. Seldom flashed- sucker! 5 QD + anchor.

51. PETE'S LEAD 5.7

40 feet up the slope, to the right of *The Vow* (#50), climb the big lieback crack to a fixed anchor.

Natural pro- mid-big sizes.

FA- Pete Story, Jeff Stallings -farming colleagues of Jim Thurmond's in SE Missouri. Jim said when he approached Pete about taking up climbing, he asked Pete how many pull-ups he could do. Pete's casual reply was, "Oh, not very many- about 2 maybe. Well, maybe 3 with my right arm".

52. EASY SLAB 5.6 TR

It's the big slab next to Route #51. Take the line of least resistance. If not, you'll easily find some 5.9ish moves. Fixed anchor on top.

53. EASY GULLY 5.6 TR

It's the gully at the right edge of *Easy Slab* (#52). Fixed anchor on top.

Continuing toward the East Falls, you'll come to a stack of cottage-size boulders. Either walk around or through them. The smooth Yosemite Slab is on the other side.

54. YOSEMITE SLAB bouldering/TR
If you traverse the broken flake to the right and step over the hallway, you can scamper up to drop a TR off the fixed belay anchor just behind the high point.

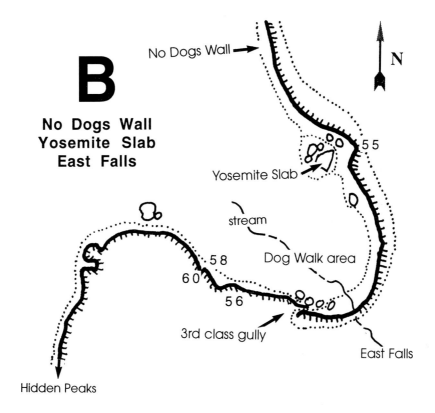

55. FREE SEX CHANGE A4
It's the thin dihedral crack right across from *Yosemite Slab*. Lorena's got nothing on this landing.

Dog Walk Area

   From Route #55, the trail continues along the bluff, then breaks away to cross the creek below the East Falls. Ten feet after crossing the creek, go left & follow the main wall to the Dog Walk gully (3rd class). There's now also a trail to the right, bypassing the gully. From the Dog Walk gully, go through the tunnel hallway & continue about 75 feet to Route #56.

56. JELLYFISH 5.7
It's the crack with a right-facing dihedral in the upper half.

57. CHUCK-O-RAMA 5.11c
Another 75 feet right, it's just left of the arete by a dihedral/off-width. 5 QD + anchor.

   About 60 feet further right is a 25-foot deep alcove.

58. SLUG MAN 5.10b
It goes up the narrow slab/face of the left, outside corner of the alcove. 3 QD + anchor

59. ACCESS DENIED 5.11a
It's the face route on the left wall in the alcove, about 15 feet left of Route #58. 4 QD + anchor

60. ESSENCE OF MANKY 5.9
It goes up the dihedral in the back of the alcove. 4 QD + anchor. Originally went out above the overhangs for a 5.11+ finish. It's often wet.

61. CREEP SHOW 5.10a
Go up the slab just right of Route #60. 3 QD + anchor.

Following the wall from here toward Hidden Peaks, you'll round a corner & head south. Just past a dead-end hallway, you'll walk beneath a 20-foot long, blank roof. About a hundred yards further south, the trail leads you between some boulders. The first one on the right features a 12-foot high, narrow arete. It points directly at *Industry* (#62).

62. INDUSTRY 5.12a
It's the overhanging face. Route angles rightward. 3 QD + anchor.

About 100 yards south of Route #62, the trail passes by some boulders that block most of your view of the cliff. A break in the middle of the boulders leads to a dihedral crack (#63) on the main wall that angles leftward. Its right side overhangs.

63. HARDY BOYS CRACK 5.9
See previous paragraph. Natural pro- small to big sizes. Fixed anchor on top. Easy TR access.

64. WATCH DOG 5.12a
About 50 feet left of Route #63, step off the small boulder & climb the face straight up, then slightly leftward. 6 QD + anchor

Hidden Peaks

The Hidden Peaks area is located at the southern end of the canyon. It consists of a portion of the main wall & 2 free-standing towers, The Monument and Pricker Peak. From Route's #63 & 64, hop back down on the trail. Continue south about 180 yards 'til you see a steep walk-up gully straight to your left. Go towards it for Routes #65 & 66.

65. DEVIL'S LAKE DREAMS 5.9
Just a bit right of the steep exit hallway leading to the top, ascend the splitter fist crack to the bulging exit moves. Natural pro- varied sizes.

66. CORAL CRACK 5.6
About 20 feet right of Route #65, go up the large, easy crack. Natural pro- varied sizes.

67. CRANIAL IMPLOSION 5.12a FA- Scott Swanson
About 25 feet left & just around the corner from Route #66, it's the overhanging face. Route angles leftward. 4 QD + anchor.

From Route #67, head to Routes #68-70 right around the corner to the big, overhanging face across from Pricker Peak.

68. ELDERS OF THE TRIBE 5.12c
It's the first sport route on the left side of the overhanging face. Definitely stiffer than the next two routes. 4 QD + anchor.

69. **DETOX MOUNTAIN** 5.12a
Way fun, tendon-friendly pump route in the middle of the wall. 6 QD + anchor.

70. **THE FARMER** 5.12a
Ascend the lieback system on the right side. 6 QD + anchor.

Pricker Peak

With your back to Routes #68-70, the following routes are listed left to right.

71. **CHEERIO BOWL** 5.10a
Start by the left corner. Follow the line up the arete. 8 QD + anchor

72. **CAPTAIN CRUNCH** 5.11c
It's the 1st sport route to the right of Route #71. 5 QD + anchor

73. **POWER PUMP** 5.10b
Just right of Route #72, ascend the broken hand-crack that angles slightly leftward to the top.
Natural pro- varied sizes

74. **ZOOM TO DOOM** 5.10b
About 15 feet right of Route #73, it's the rounded corner.
Natural pro- varied sizes

The Monument

With your back to the main wall, these routes are also listed left to right.

75. **MONUMENTAL FEAR** 5.8 X lead or TR
About 5 feet around the left corner, go straight up. Route was the original access route to the top.

76. **LOTHLORIEN** 5.10a
Ascend the middle of the face. <u>Mixed pro</u>- 4 QD, TCU's + anchor.

77. **NAKED BLADE** 5.11a
On the right corner, ascend the 90 degree arete.
<u>Mixed pro</u>- 4 QD, small Friend & Tri-cams, + anchor.

78. **THE JUGGLER** 5.12a
Right around the corner from Route #77, go up the middle of the wall, then follow the crack to the top. <u>Mixed pro</u>- 5 QD, Friends + anchor.

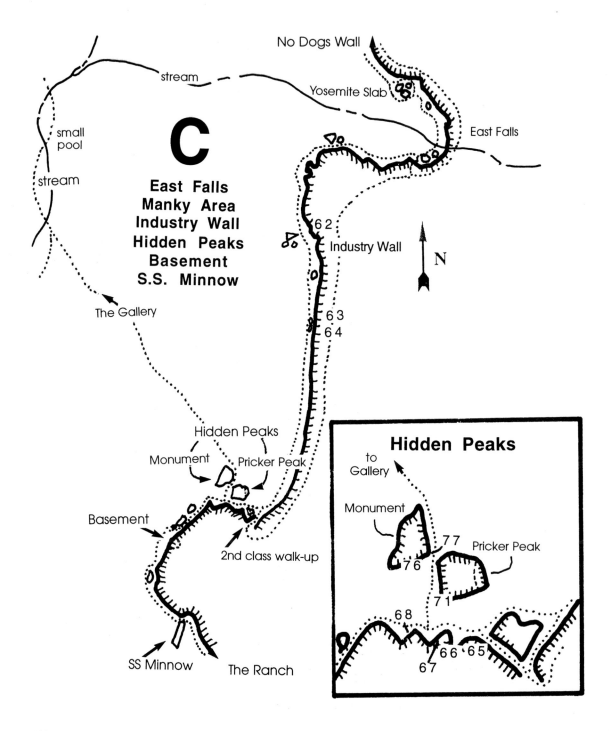

No Dogs Wall

stream

Yosemite Slab

East Falls

small
pool

stream

C

**East Falls
Manky Area
Industry Wall
Hidden Peaks
Basement
S.S. Minnow**

6 2

Industry Wall

N

The Gallery

6 3
6 4

Hidden Peaks

Monument

Pricker Peak

Basement

2nd class walk-up

SS Minnow

The Ranch

Hidden Peaks

to
Gallery

Monument

7 7

Pricker Peak

7 6

7 1

6 8

7 7 6 6 6 5

6 7

The Basement

The Basement, a 25-foot long, 45 degree overhang on the main wall is approximately 220 yards further south past the Hidden Peaks.

79. **PROJECT**
Left side of the overhang.

80. **MISERY** 5.13a
It goes up the middle of the overhang. 2 QD + anchor.

81. **COUP D'ETAT** 5.13a
Ascend the right side of the overhang & continue through the upper wall. 8 QD + anchor.

S.S. Minnow

The S.S. Minnow, another free-standing tower, is located about 150 yards past The Basement. Follow the cliff as it bends around to face westward. As you approach the S.S. Minnow, you'll see its obvious ship appearance.

82. **THREE HOUR TOUR** 5.10a
It's the face route that follows the edge of the ship's bow. Start off of the boulders, then traverse left toward the corner. 5 QD + anchor.

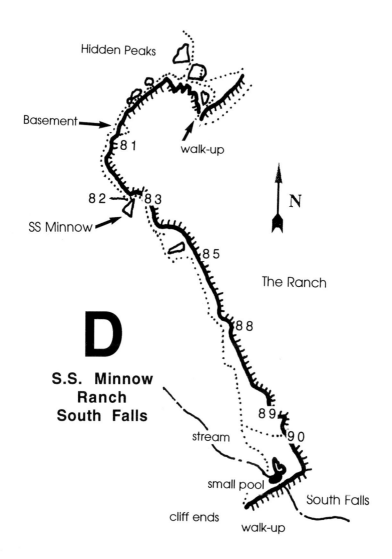

Hidden Peaks

Basement

81

walk-up

N

82 → 83

SS Minnow →

85

The Ranch

D

88

**S.S. Minnow
Ranch
South Falls**

stream

89

90

small pool

South Falls

cliff ends

walk-up

The Ranch

The Ranch area begins on the main wall, just past the S.S. Minnow.

83. **SPACE COWBOY** 5.12b
About 30 feet past the S.S. Minnow, it starts just right of the big, overhung dihedral. Cross the crack after the 2nd clip & face climb through the bulge to the top. 8 QD + anchor.
GANGSTER OF LOVE variation 5.12c- tops out left to separate anchor. 8 QD + anchor.

Continue about 60 yards further south of the S.S. Minnow. You'll walk past large boulders. The trail then hooks to meet the cliff at a vertical groove/gully, Route #85.

84. <u>BRIEF RESPITE</u> 5.8
It's 40 feet left of Route #85. Take the slab just right of a right-slanting crack. 5 QD + anchor.

85. <u>GROOVY MARCIA!</u> 5.9
Go up the groove. The trail takes you right to it. 6 QD + anchor.

86. <u>DISCO FEVER</u> 5.12c
It starts about 10 feet right of Route #85. 7 QD + anchor.

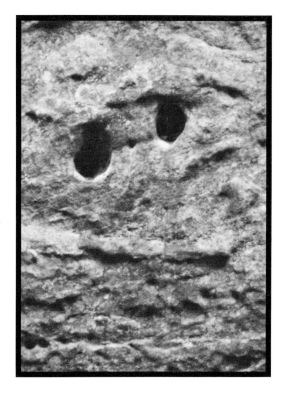

87. <u>LASSO THE VULTURE</u> 5.11a
About 15 feet right of Route #86, ascend the face. Top out through the gully that marks the left edge of a 12-foot blank roof. 7 QD + anchor.

88. <u>CONDOR</u> 5.11c
About 50 feet right of Route #87, ascend the arete, just right of a stem crack. 5 QD + anchor

After about 100 yards, the trail drifts away from the cliff. For Route #89, cut up toward the cliff to a short, overhanging bulge split by a flaring crack.

89. <u>SOUTHERN INQUISITION</u> 5.10b
Go up the left side of the overhanging bulge. 5 QD + anchor

Routes #90 & 91 start about 60 feet right of Route #9. They parallel up the overhanging face & share a common anchor.

90. <u>COWBOYS & CROSS DRESSERS</u> 5.12a
It's the left route. 4 QD + anchor.

91. <u>DARWIN'S THEORY</u> 5.12b
Go up the right side route. 4 QD + anchor.

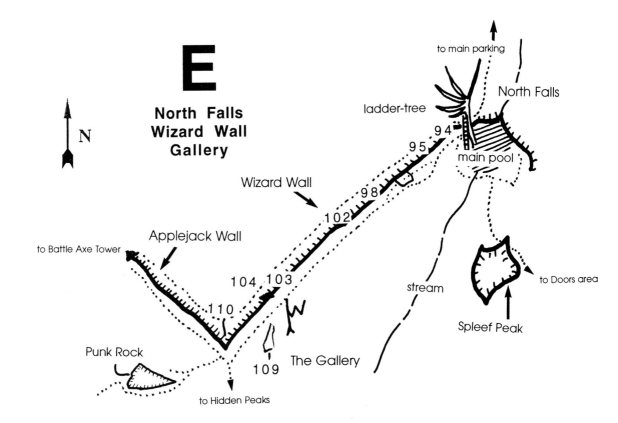

Ladder-Tree Area

Routes starting left (listed right to left as you're facing the cliff) of the main waterfall...

92. **HUECOOL** 5.11b TR
Start a few feet <u>right</u> of the ladder-tree. Go straight up.

93. **CUJO** 5.10b TR
Start 5 feet left of the ladder-tree. Go straight up.

Routes #94 & 95 were established during Thanksgiving break, 1987, while camping in Leprosy Cave during a 4-day rainstorm. The only way to dry out was to stand in the smoke of the fire. Now there was a vacation.

94. **LOVIN' LIZARDS** 5.7+ TR
About 50 feet left of the ladder-tree, ascend the slab just prior to the corner. Fixed anchor on top.

95. **TEMPORARY ESCAPE** 5.10d
It's opposite the corner from Route
#94. 3 QD + anchor.

96. **BUG MEAT** 5.10a
Goes up just left of Route #95.
Funky start.
Mixed pro- 2 QD, TCU's or Tri-cams
+ anchor.

97. **EAT DIRT** 5.10a w/Sorel boots
Nasty off-width left of *Bug Meat*
(#96). In a fit of climbing fever in
mid-winter, Michael donned his Sorel
boots and cranked the route, using a
TCU in the snow-filled crack for
good looks.
FA- Michael Simpson '87

Wizard Wall

98. **WIZARD'S HAT** 5.10b
Just past a leaning boulder, ascend the crack in the back of an overhanging, symmetrical dihedral.
Natural pro- varied sizes FA went on Halloween weekend of '85.
variation (5.9+ TR)- ascend the flakes to the right.

99. **SETTLED CONTROVERSY** 5.9
Starts behind a VW Bug-size rock. Ascend the big lieback flake with a horn on top. Top out up
and right.
Mixed pro- small nut, mid-size Friend, 2 QD + anchor.
FA- Lawrence Stuemke, Tim Scuras '88 Lawrence led it without fixed pro. Pretty bold!

100. **WHAT, HOW?** 5.10 TR
Just left of Route #99, it's the deep and dirty dihedral capped by a small roof.

101. **SUSPENDED ANIMATION** 5.9
About 75 feet left of Route's #99 & 100, it's the route with a crack in the middle. Route strays right at the top. Top out straight for a harder variation. <u>Mixed pro</u>- 2 QD, mid size, + anchor.

102. **DECEPTION** 5.10b
25 feet left of Route #101, fire up the dihedral crack next to a low roof. <u>Natural pro</u>- small-mid size + anchor.

The Gallery

From *Deception* (#102), the trail drops down a steep section, below Leprosy Cave up to the right. It then rises up a slope where there's a W-shape tree opposite a big chimney.

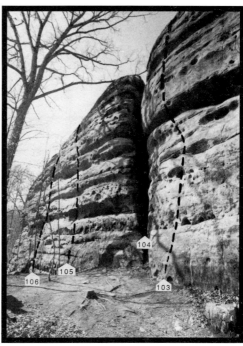

103. <u>THE MINSTREL</u> 5.10c
It's just right of the chimney. 4 QD + anchor.

104. **THE CRINGE CHIMNEY** 5.6 TR
It's the big chimney.

105. <u>YUPPIE WITH A GUN</u> 5.11a
1st route left of *The Cringe Chimney* (#104). 4 QD + anchor.
FA- Michael Simpson '87 name inspired by deer season- Michael thought he may have to dodge bullets since he was without any hunter orange lycra.

106. **KING'S JESTER** 5.11a
Start on the big crack just left of *Yuppie* (#105). Go up through the vertical seam. Bottom can protect with stoppers. 3 QD + anchor.
variation 5.10- stay 6 feet right of the vertical seam to the slab.

107. **THE UNBOLTED ONE** 5.10b
Start on *King's Jester* (#106). Angle up and left through the pocketed face.
Natural pro- Big Bro's
FA- John Sherman on-sight (could've guessed, eh?), Michael Simpson '89

108. **EARTHBOUND MISFIT** 5.10b TR
Just prior to turning the 90 degree corner, ascend the pocketed face straight up.
FA- Lawrence Stuemke '88 A misnomer as he's a successful climbing guide in Colorado.

109. **MR. ROGERS** Kids' Climb
Small boulder directly in front of *King's Jester*. Ascend the pocketed vertical section.
FA- Phillip Carrier 1993

110. **PSYCHOTHERAPY** 5.10c
Just left of Route #108, ascend the sport route on the corner. 7 QD + anchor.

111. **GROUP THERAPY** 5.10b very popular
It's the overhanging jug haul just around the 90 degree corner. 6 QD + anchor.
FA- Alan Carrier and a group of fine folk '89

112. **SQUIRREL HOUSE CRACK** 5.9
Overhung crack just left of *Group Therapy* (#111). Top out on #111 or #113.
Natural pro- bring TCU's for sure.
FA- John Payne '86 As John was pulling up to the shelf, a startled squirrel dove out of the crack, right by John's face. It tumbled end over end a couple times, then righted itself just in time to catch a branch & run away.

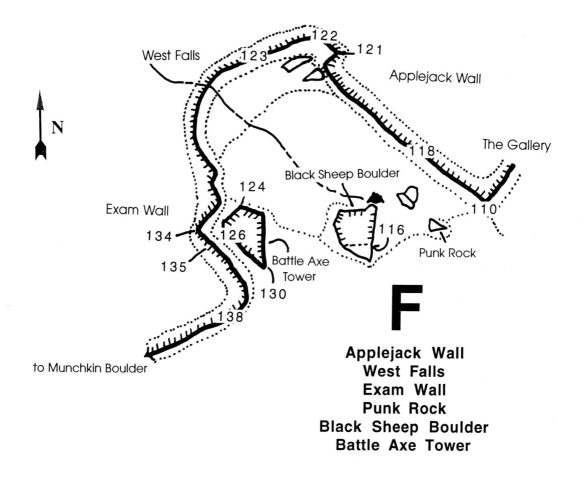

F

Applejack Wall
West Falls
Exam Wall
Punk Rock
Black Sheep Boulder
Battle Axe Tower

113. **SHOCK THERAPY** 5.12a
Starts 5 feet left of Route #112. 5 QD + anchor.

Punk Rock

Kids' Climbs. Punk Rock is a 15 foot high boulder directly below *Group Therapy* (#111) that sports 2 short top rope problems. Both routes face *Group Therapy*. The only two sizable trees visible at the top edge mark the routes.

114. **LEFT ROUTE** 5.3
Big holds to the top.

115. **RIGHT ROUTE** 5.3
More big holds to the top.

Black Sheep Boulder

It's the next free-standing tower below Punk Rock.

116. <u>TOUCH MY SHELF</u> 5.12a
As you approach the Black Sheep Boulder, it's the route going up the right side of the steep overhang. 5 QD + anchor.

117. <u>ENERGIZER</u> 5.12a
Walk all the way around Black Sheep Boulder. It goes up just left of an arete. 5 QD + anchor.

AppleJack Wall

Continuing leftward, down the main wall from Route #113...

118. **APPLEJACK CRACK** 5.11b
Next to a large tree, ascend the thin crack that turns into a solution off-width.
<u>Natural pro</u>- all sizes + anchor.
FA- Eric Ulner '85 Anticipating hunger while I would belay Miguel Balaguero as he cleaned the pitch, I stuck an apple in my back pocket. I didn't anticipate shoving that side of my butt into the crack, however. Past the crux & feeling moisture seeping through my pants, I announced to Miguel that the apple was jacked, whereby I threw it to the ground. Miguel, apparently hungrier than I, picked it up & commenced eating its good side. Just thought you'd like to know.

John Payne on *Group Therapy*, Jackson Falls

Interpretation of stone swirls, Jackson Falls

Routes #119 & 120 start about 35 feet off the ground.

119. **THE SHOOTIST** 5.12a (rap in)
It's about 30 feet left of Route #118. Rappel straight down to a fixed belay anchor (50 meter rope will reach the ground). Have a QD in hand and don't lose your swing!
<u>Mixed pro</u>- 5 QD, a mid-size TCU for a horizontal slot near the top, + anchor.

120. **CORPORAL PUNISHMENT** 5.11a (rap in) It's about 30 feet left of *The Shootist* (#119). Angle slightly rightward while you're rappelling to the fixed belay anchor. Don't get spanked!
<u>Mixed pro</u>- 2 QD, small nuts, Friends, + anchor.

120A. **BILL & TEE'S EXCELLENT ADVENTURE** 5.10b kinda reachy
Go up the arete down to the left of Route #120. Route starts off the ledge. 5 QD + anchor.

121. **BUCKETS OF JAM** 5.8
It's the big dihedral crack to the left.
<u>Natural pro</u>- varied sizes.

122. **RAGIN' CAJUN** 5.12c
Further up the slope to the left, very tricky face moves take you to a pumpin', overhung exit. 7 QD + anchor.

Michael Simpson on *Rajin' Cajun*

123. INFERNO 5.12a TR
Just prior to the West Falls, do the lie-back system in front of a large boulder.
FA- Jim Thurmond '88 FA went up by the light of a sizable midnite campfire at the base. Jim would call out, "more leaves"! as he would need light.

West Falls below

Battle Axe Tower

The Battle Axe is the next free-standing tower past the West Falls. Inside the hallway are some of the most majestic trees (Poplar, I've been told) in the hollow.

124. **WRECKING BALL** 5.12c
It's the overhanging arete on your left, prior to entering the hallway. Your body will tend to act like a wrecking ball if you peel off this one. Also sports a classy, no feet clip. 6 QD + anchor.

125. **DOS HOMBRES** 5.10a kinda reachy
Easy moves to a flat-top block mark this arete route. 3 QD + anchor up in tree.

126. **VIKING BLOOD** 5.12c
Around the corner in the hallway, it's the left side of the sheer-looking face.
5 QD + anchor up in tree.

127. **THE FLAIL** 5.12d
It goes up the right side of the face. 6 QD + anchor.

128. **CROSS-EYED MARY** 5.12c TR
Start on Route #127. Angle up & right, topping out on #129.

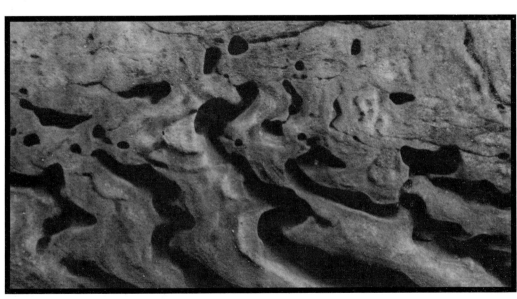

Looking back into the Battle Axe hallway

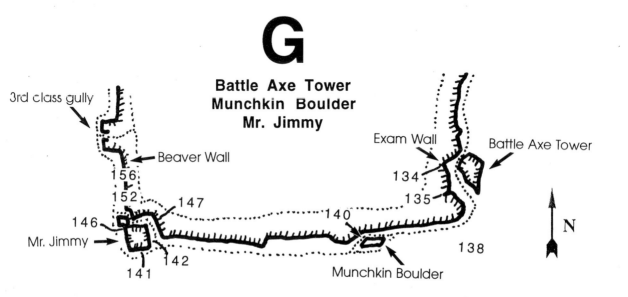

G

Battle Axe Tower
Munchkin Boulder
Mr. Jimmy

129. **THE DAGGER** 5.8 X
Foot-traverse rightward along the lip of the knee-level roof to the arete. Go straight up to the ledge. Natural pro- small sizes. The gear sucks.

130. **VOID WARRIOR** 5.11d
Step around the corner of the Battle Axe Tower, out of the hallway. It goes up the left side of the face. 5 QD + anchor.

Exam Wall

The Exam Wall begins across the hallway from the Battle Axe Tower.

131. **BURSTING OUT** 5.12c
Opposite of Route #125 & to the right of the big off-width, it's the thin face topped by a 3-foot roof. Pretty airy above the roof. 6 QD + anchor.

132. **THE OFF-WIDTH EXAM** 5.12a TR
It's the big off-width starting in an overhanging symmetrical dihedral. Gee, have fun.
FA- Jim Thurmond '87 "Just breathe in & stick, then exhale & move an inch. Repeat".

133. **EAST OF EAST ST. LOUIS** 5.13b
Just left of *The Off-Width Exam* (#132), it's extremely thin face, overhung at the top. Way hard is putting it mildly. Stand with your back touching the base & look up for the breathtaking effect. 6 QD + anchor.

134. **THE BOLTED ONE** 5.11d
It's the huge dihedral crack. The 1st route in the canyon to receive a safety-bolt. For months, it was referred to as the bolted one. The name stuck. Awesome stemming.
Mixed pro- varied sizes, 1 QD + anchor. Upper half takes wires nicely.

135. **BEAVER BONES** 5.9 R
About 60 feet left of *The Bolted One* (#134), ascend the left-facing dihedral crack. A beaver skeleton was found at the base of the route.
Natural pro- small stuff + anchor. Better know what you're doing.

136. **THE SOPHOMORE** 5.9 (translation- The Wise Fool)
It goes up about 20 feet left of *Beaver Bones* (#135). Mixed pro- varied sizes, 3 QD + anchor.

137. **TONS OF FUN** 5.10d
About 5 feet left of Route #136, go up the face & through the overhang at the top. 6 QD + anchor.

Follow the trail around the bend to where the cliff faces south.

138. **EMPEROR OF THE NORTH** 5.13a
It's the 1st route around the bend past the Battle Axe Tower. Heinous and steep pocket pulling. Stick clip. 6 QD + anchor.

139. PROJECT smells like 13+
Cuts left after the 2nd clip on *Emperor of the North* (#138). Open to all.

The Munchkin Boulder

     The Munchkin Boulder is the 25-foot high, free-standing block to the left of *Emperor of the North* (#138). The main wall across its hallway sports a tendon-friendly warm-up traverse.

140. THE MUNCHKIN 5.9
It's the short route on the high point of the block inside the hallway. 2 QD + anchor.

Random bouldering along the trail to
Mr. Jimmy

Mr. Jimmy

Mr. Jimmy is the next free-standing tower about 250 yards west of The Munchkin Boulder. You'll pass good bouldering along the way.

141. <u>DON'T MESS WITH THE BULL</u> 5.12b
Look to left of the Mr. Jimmy hallway entrance. It's the first route on the outside of the tower. 5 QD + anchor.

142. <u>VENOM</u> 5.10a
As you enter the hallway, it's the 1st route on your left. 7 QD + anchor.

143. <u>STINGER</u> 5.10b
It's just right of *Venom* (#142). Traverse the long shelf near the top. Top out on *Venom* (#142). 6 QD + anchor.

144. <u>STINGER DIRECT</u> 5.11a/b
Take *Stinger* to its own anchor. 6 QD + anchor.

145. <u>VOICE</u> 5.12d
It starts just right of Route #144. Traverse to the arete and go up. It really is a beautiful line. 8 QD + anchor.

146. <u>SPIRIT</u> 5.12a
Continue around the corner from *Voice* (#145). Scramble up the boulder to begin the route over the hallway. 4 QD + anchor.

Back on the main wall across the hallway from Route #145...

147. **OFF WEB** 5.7
It's the off-width to the right of the slab/corner. The right side of it is sharp and incut.

148. **SCREAMERY** 5.4
Left of *Off Web* (#147), ascend the dihedral slab.

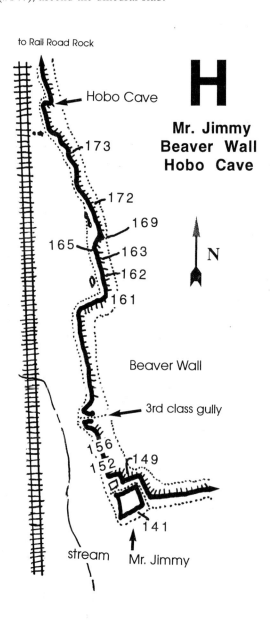

to Rail Road Rock

Hobo Cave

H

**Mr. Jimmy
Beaver Wall
Hobo Cave**

173

172

169

165

163

N

162

161

Beaver Wall

3rd class gully

156

152   149

141

stream   Mr. Jimmy

149. **LUSCIOUS BABES** 5.8

Still in the hallway, it's the long, clean slab right down to the left of Route #148. Usually a TR, although Barb led it with a piece or two. Fixed anchor. Fun route.
FA- Barbara Knowles, Lisa Verkler '90

150. **THIN LIZZY** 5.12a TR

Continuing through the hallway past Route #149, turn right into a narrower hallway. On the boulder to your left, climb just to the right of the center of the face. You'll be below *Spirit* (#146).

151. **LUCKY BASTARD** 5.9

It's the crack in the 90 degree dihedral on the main wall, 6 feet right of *Thin Lizzy* (#150).
FSA- Jim Thurmond '89. How many times does this one make?

Beaver Wall

Beaver Wall begins at the overhung section, just past Mr. Jimmy.

152. TASMANIAN DEVIL 5.12b
Go up the right side of the overhang. Go straight above the last QD so the tree won't be a threat. Bad opinions of the route usually made by people who can't do it. 4 QD + anchor.

153. EVERYBODY NEEDS FRIENDS 5.12a
Angle leftward on *Tasmanian Devil.* 4 QD + anchor.

154. FRIZZLE FRY 5.12b
1st route left of Route #153. Trickier than it looks. 5 QD + anchor.

155. SHORTY THE PIMP 5.13a
Just left of *Frizzle Fry.* 5 QD + anchor.

156. WHO NEEDS FRIENDS? 5.12a
Just left of Route #155, do the leftward slanting crack.

157. RED CORVETTE 5.13a
It's just left of Route #156. 5 QD + anchor.

158. PROJECT

159. FLINGIN' HOG 5.10c (translation-expelling expired tobacco flavored worm dirt)
Go up the right side of the arete at the left end of the overhang. 7 QD + anchor
FA- John & Maria Sommerhof, Geoff Thorsen, Kerby McGhee '92. Sounds like a real party. By the way- to fling one's hog, one must first

determine that the hog has become defunct. If so, insert a crooked forefinger in between the lower lip & gum line (if there's one left), then sweep out the hog with the finger & give it a good snap of the wrist in order to fling with expertise. Be careful with wrist whiplash so as not to get any hog in your eye.

Up a rise in the trail past *Flingin' Hog* (#159) is a 3rd class gully to the top. A bit further and around the corner, you'll come to a large dihedral crack, *Chit Chat* (#161).

160. GET OUT OF MY KITCHEN 5.10c
Take the arching crack into *Chit Chat* (#161).
<u>Natural pro-</u> varied sizes, bring Friends.

161. **CHIT CHAT** 5.7
It's the large dihedral crack in the corner.
Natural pro- varied sizes

162. **MARY'S COOKIES** 5.11d
In front of a big boulder about 35 feet left of *Chit Chat* (#161), it goes up a high angle slab with a thin face crack at the base. 6 QD + anchor. John was having trouble with the crux until he was fired up by some of Mary Dippie's sugar cookies. Nothing like a good sugar buzz.
FA- John Payne '87

163. **BIRTHDAY ROUTE** 5.10b
About 100 feet left of *Mary's Cookies* (#162), ascend the semi-pillar between 2 prominent gullies.
7 QD + anchor.

164. **EXPRESS CHECKOUT LINE** 5.10a
It starts about 10 left of Route #163. 7 QD + anchor.

165. **MANUFACTURER'S CONSENT** 5.13a
It's the 1st route on the corner left of Route #164. Veer right at the 2nd clip. 8 QD + anchor.

166. **ZEN ARCADE** 5.13b
Same start as Route #165. Go straight up at the 2nd clip. 9 QD + anchor. WOW.

167. **WORKING CLASS** 5.12d
It's the next route left of Route #166. Starts out on eye bolts. 10 QD + anchor.

168. **GOBBLE JUICE** 5.12d
Next route left of *Working Class* (#167). 10 QD + anchor

169. **NO NAME DIHEDRAL** 5.9
It's the prominent dihedral to the left of *Gobble Juice* (#168).

About another 100 feet past *No Name Dihedral* (#169) is a stack of large boulders. Behind them is a dihedral crack capped by a blank, 4-foot roof, *No Paynes in Heaven*.

170. **MASON-DIXON LINE** 5.12c
2nd sport route to the right of Route #172. 6 QD + anchor.

171. **RAGING INTENSITY** 5.12a
Arete route just right of Route #172. 6 QD + anchor.

172. **NO PAYNES IN HEAVEN** 5.10c R
Climb the dihedral. Exit left of the roof through the crack. Natural pro- varied sizes
FA- John Payne '87 nyuck nyuck

173. **AFTER-HOURS** 5.9
About 50 yards left of Route #172, locate a broken, right-facing dihedral system capped by a roof with a ramp above it. Pitch 1- Climb the crack for about 25 feet and traverse leftward across the 1st ledge. Take the crack above there to the base of the ramp and belay. Pich 2- Go up the ramp and top out.
Natural pro- varied sizes

Hobo Cave

The trail forks just past *After-Hours* (#173). A right turn will take you along the wall to Hobo Cave.

174. **LIVING ON THE EDGE** 5.12d
It's the rightmost route of the Hobo Cave. 5 QD + anchor.

175. **PROJECT**

176. **ANIMAL HUSBANDRY** 5.12c
It goes up the left edge of Hobo Cave. Take the right top-out. 6 QD + anchor.

177. **BELCHING FIANCE** 5.12a
same as *Animal Husbandry* (#176). Take the left top-out. 6 QD + anchor.

Continue following the cliff line for about 100 yards. Routes #178 & 179 are about 50 feet prior to Railroad Rock hallway.

178. **SWEEPER** 5.8
Just right of *Creeper Dihedral* (# 179), ascend the slanted dihedral ramp to where a shelf system cuts back left. Take the shelf and exit to a ledge above it.

179. **CREEPER DIHEDRAL** 5.9
It's the right-facing dihedral with a perfect crack.
Natural pro- mid sizes

The following routes start on the main wall in the Rail Road Rock hallway.

180. **PERMISSION DENIED** 5.12a
It's the 1st route on the main wall across the hallway from RR Rock. It's just right of a large tree.
6 QD + anchor.

181. **BUTCHER OF BAGHDAD** 5.13a
It starts about 15 feet left of the tree next to *Permission Denied* (#180). Very thin face. 6 QD + anchor. Very technical.

182. **NO NAME DIHEDRAL** 5.7
Obvious dihedral crack in the hallway.
Natural pro- big stuff.

183. **SLAB STICK COMEDY** 5.12a
Slab sport route left of the dihedral. Often causes whining & brooding. 4 QD + anchor.

184. **KISS THAT FROG** 5.12a TR
Start at the base of the off-width left of *Slab Stick Comedy* (#183). Go up left and ascend the middle of the face.

185. **TOP OF THE MORNING TO YOU** 5.12b
Walk northward out of R.R. Rock hallway. Turn right at the corner and look up. 4 QD.

186. **MOTHER'S DAY SPECIAL** 5.10c
Start at the slanted crack, left of Route #185. Take the route as it goes up & left. 5 QD + anchor.

187. **CHEAP FAME** 5.11d
About 50 left of Route #186, ascend the shallow gully. 4 QD + anchor.

Railroad Rock

188. **SUNNY SIDE** 5.8 TR
On the RR Rock, it's the vertical gully in the middle of the side facing the tracks.

189. **ELECTROCUTIONER** 5.8+ TR
To the right of *Sunny Side* (#188), it's the rounded arete. Shouldn't take too much to figure out this one's name.

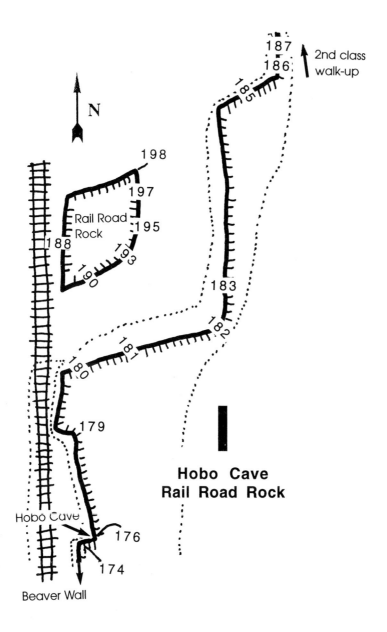

N

187
186
↑ 2nd class walk-up

185

198
197
Rail Road Rock
195
188
193
190

183
182

181
180

179

■

Hobo Cave
Rail Road Rock

Hobo Cave
176
174

Beaver Wall

190. FRAGILE EGOS/INTO THE SUN 5.10d
It's the 1st sport route on your left as you enter the hallway from the tracks. 7 QD + anchor.
FA- Jane Sparboro '81 Jane called it *Fragile Egos* following rude comments from the male peanut gallery down below, many of whom couldn't do the route.
1st Free Lead- Rob Drysdale '90 Unaware of Jane's ascent, Rob opened one of the hollow's most enjoyable sport routes, calling it *Into the Sun*.

Eric Ulner on *Butcher of Baghdad*, Jackson Falls

John Yaworsky on *Mary's Cookies,* Jackson Falls

191. BARBARIANS AT THE GATE
5.12a
Just right of *Fragile Egos* (#190). 7 QD + anchor.

192. DAMN YANKEES 5.12a TR
Ascend the leftward arching arete/face in between Route #191.

193. WHERE'S MY BOURBON? 5.12b
It goes up the rightward arching arete.
6 QD + anchor.

194. BLUE VELVET 5.11d
Sport route just right of *Bourbon* (#193).
5 QD + anchor.
FA- Rich Bechler, Rob Drysdale '90
Dedicated to Rob Drysdale, who was fatally injured in 1992 while bouldering in Arizona.

195. WILD AT HEART 5.11b
It's just right of *Blue Velvet* (#194).
Traverse the ledge rightward or gun it up and left to exit. 5 QD + anchor.

196. AMERICAN HANDGUNNER
5.12a
Next route right of Route #195. Finish at Route #195. 5 QD + anchor.

Read the train. Now there's timing!

197. THE DRIFTER 5.11a
Sport route just left of the Route #198. 5 QD + anchor.

198. TRAIN! 5.10b
Ascend the arete at the north end of the hallway. 5 QD + anchor.

CLIMBING ROUTE INDEXES

by difficulty grade, with first ascent (FA) credits
First ascents not listed are unknown.

FOUNTAIN BLUFF

GIANT CITY STATE PARK

Shelter #1 Bluff

Devil's Standtable area

CEDAR BLUFF

DRAPER'S BLUFF

FERNE CLYFFE STATE PARK

**TECHNICAL, NO-HANDS
CLIMBING**

JACKSON FALLS cont.

SAMPLE CLIMBING FOR TOTS

Glossary

This glossary is for term and jargon familiarity, not instructional purposes.

Aid Climbing- the direct use of equipment for means of ascent; grabbing-pulling-stepping on rope, sling, hardware, etc.

Anchor- refers to natural or fixed protection placed in the rock for the purposes of belaying or protecting the leader while climbing. Term refers to *belay anchor* in this guide.

Arete- a protruding ridge or spine of rock.

Bail gear- when a leader has to back off of a route, it's the protection left in the rock for lowering/rappel purposes.

Belayer- the person who controls the rope and the friction device by either giving or removing slack from the rope as the climber requires.

Big Bro- a type of natural protection.

Bluff scalin'- climbing. *"You'nzer crazy doin' that thar bluff scalin'!"*

Bomber- secure; *bomber handhold, bomber pro.*

Bouldering- to climb/traverse without a rope usually no more than 15 feet in height.

Bucket- an easy to grab, large hold.

Cams- protection that works on a camming principle.

Chalk- for drying the hands. Same stuff gymnasts use.

Chimney- a crack with enough width to accommodate a person

Choss- nasty, breakable rock.

Crater- see Grounder.

Crux- the hardest move(s) on a route.

Deck- as in, "to deck"- see Grounder.

Dihedral- an inside corner formed at the juncture of two planes or surfaces (of rock). Around here, there's nearly always a crack at the juncture.

Duck butt- an incompetent climber who doesn't think so; see "Wallydraigle".

Ego Whine- sound sometimes associated with removal of first ascent credits in guidebooks

FA- first ascent.

FSA- first solo ascent.

Fixed anchor- In this guide, refers to "fixed belay anchor".

Fixed pro- protection placed in the rock with the intent of it's staying there, such as a pin or safety-bolt. Although, natural pro can also become fixed after receiving a hard fall. The decision is yours when using any fixed pro.

Flash- a successful, no-falls ascent on the 1st attempt.

Free climbing- to climb without direct assistance of equipment; rope, slings, etc., used for safety, not for grabbing.

Free solo climbing - to climb without a safety-rope. Term usually applied to a climber in or above spinal zone.

Friend- the original SLCD.

Ground up- a style of opening a route. Any fixed protection is placed while leading as opposed to on rappel.

Grounder- ground fall- to hit the ground.

Hex- a type of natural protection that works on a wedging or camming principle.

Holler- a rural, dialectical pronunciation for hollow.

Hueco- Spanish term used for pockets.

Jug- see Bucket.

Leader fall- a fall taken while leading; term used when the last protection placed is below the leader. Leader fall = (2 x run-out length) + any stretch + any slack.

Micro- a small hold.

Mixed pro- for this guidebook, it refers to a combination of fixed and natural protection.

Mono- usually refers to a one-finger pocket, not the sickness.

Natural line- a route that accepts the use of natural pro.

Natural pro- removable pro, such as wedging or camming devices.

Necky- possibly dangerous; as in, sticking your neck out for something.

Nuclear- see Bomber

Numb nut- see Duck butt.

Off-width- a crack too wide for a fist jam and too narrow for chimney technique- "awful width"

On-sight- to climb with no prior knowledge of the route, whether it be visual pre-inspection or verbal description. A misnomer for routes with obvious chalk or tick marks.

Oogies- the sensation of spinal chills induced by fear.

Open- to do the 1st ascent of a route.

Open book gully- a gully resembling the inside gutter of an open book.

Pin- piton.

Pink-point- a successful, no-falls lead ascent of a route that has preplaced protection rigged with carabiners.

Pitch- the distance of rock climbed from one belay to the next.

PPFFT- the sound of a startled frog landing 75 feet below.

Pro- protection. Any anchor used to safeguard the lead climber.

Propellin'- Rappelling. Term coined by curious onlooker. "Are you'nz propellin' up that bluff?"

QD- see quickdraw.

Quickdraw- 2 carabiners joined by a short piece of webbing, primarily used for fixed protection.

R- attached to a route's number grade if there is a potentially injurious, long fall.

Red Point- a successful, no-falls lead ascent of a route, not necessarily on-sight.

Roof- an intimidating part of the cliff that sticks out like a ceiling.

Route- a climb.

Run-out- the distance between you and your previous piece of pro on a lead climb. The term is more often used when the distance is great (huh? great?).

SLCD- spring loaded camming device; a type of natural pro.

Safety-bolts- a type of fixed (but not forever safe) pro used when natural pro is inadequate or nonexistent.

Slab- a less than vertical rock face.

Slingshot TR- term is mostly used in a single-pitch environment of 80 feet in height or less. The rope runs from the climber, up the cliff, through an anchor, then down to the belayer on the ground. See Top-Rope

Spinal zone- when bouldering high or free-soloing, the height reached where spinal injury is likely if a fall were to occur. Definitely your call, though.

Sport climbing- lead climbing on routes equipped with fixed protection, usually safety-bolts. The protection is usually placed in such a manner so as to reduce ground-fall potential.

Spotter- one who spots a climber, usually when bouldering. Spotting can include literally catching a falling climber or slightly breaking his/her fall, or simply making sure the falling climber's head does not hit the ground.

Spring Huecos- Road potholes in the spring.

Stance- usually refers to the position maintained on the rock while placing protection or rigging a belay on a lead climb.

Stick clip- a method of clipping the 1st pro on a route prior to leaving the ground. A stick is employed, although sometimes shinnying a nearby tree works too.

TCU- three cam unit; a type of natural protection.

TR- top-rope

Top out- to climb the final or exit moves of a route.

Top-rope- a safety system used whereby a rope is tied to the climber's harness and runs above the climber through an anchored friction device. The rope may also be redirected through an anchor, above the belayer (see Slingshot TR).

Trad- traditional, natural protection

Traverse- to climb sideways.

Varied pro- a mixture of sizes from small to large.

Wallydraigle- a slovenly creature.

Whip jag- see Duck butt.

Whipper- a fairly lengthy leader fall.

X- attached to a route's number grade if cratering or hitting a ledge is likely during a lead fall.

Jackson on *No Thumbs Allowed,* Opie's Kitchen

BLACK DIAMOND EQUIPMENT.
READY WHEN YOU ARE.

2084 EAST 3900 SOUTH, SALT LAKE CITY, UT 84124 USA (801) 278-5533
PHOTO BY KEVIN POWELL

CLIMBING GYMS & SERVICES

ILLINOIS

BELLEVILLE YMCA
15 N. 1st Street
Belleville, IL 62220-1394
618-233-1243

HIDDEN PEAK
937 W. Chestnut
Chicago, IL 60622
312-563-9400

UPPER LIMITS
1304 W. Washington
Bloomington, IL 61701
309-829-2284

VERTICAL HEARTLAND CLIMBING SCHOOL
Makanda, IL
618-549-1189 phone/fax

VERTICAL PLAINS
25 E. Springfield Ave.
Champaign, IL 61820
217-356-2412

MICHIGAN

PLANET ROCK
34 Rapid St.
Pontiac, MI 48342
810-334-3904

MISSOURI

THE GOOD LIFE
All American Indoor
Sports Mall
111 33rd Lindberg Bus. Ct.
St. John's Church Rd.
St. Louis, MO
314-845-3656

RETAILERS

ILLINOIS

ACTIVE ENDEAVORS
935 W. Armitage
Chicago, IL 60614
312-281-8100
&
1527 Chicago Ave.
Evanston, IL 60201
708-869-7073

THE NORTH FACE
416 Oakbrook Center
Oakbrook, IL 60521
708-990-0303
&
Woodfield Mall
Schaumburg, IL
708-240-1725
&
Chicago, IL
312-337-7200

WILD COUNTRY
612 S. Neil
Champaign, IL 61820-4340
217-351-4754
&
203 S. Linden
Normal, IL 61761
309-452-0222

INDIANA

JL WATER'S & CO.
109 N. College St.
Bloomington, IN 47401
812-334-1845

LAKE & LAND OUTFITTERS
64 Lincoln Way
Valparaiso, IN 46383
219-464-9006

IOWA

ACTIVE ENDEAVORS
9747 University Ave.
Clive, IA 50325
515-226-9345
&
138 S. Clinton
Iowa City, IA 52240
319-337-9444

KENTUCKY

HANK BROS. TRUE VALUE
3101 Lone Oak Rd.
Paducah, KY 42003
502-554-4001

MISSOURI

ALPINE SHOP
601 E. Lockwood
Webster Groves, MO 63119
314-962-7715

BACKWOODS
12366 Olive Blvd.
St. Louis, MO 63141
314-878-1618

SMITH SPORTING GOODS
111 W. Lockwood
Webster Groves, MO 63119
314-961-4742

TENNESSEE

OUTDOORS, INC.
5245 Poplar Ave.
Memphis, TN 38119
901-767-6790

WISCONSIN

ACTIVE ENDEAVORS
341 State St.
Madison, WI 53703
608-257-8500

EQUIPMENT COMPANIES

BLACK DIAMOND
2084 E. 3900 South
Salt Lake City, UT 84124
801-278-5533

MOUNTAIN GEAR
2002 N. Division
Spokane, WA 99207
800-829-2009

ROCKTONICS
171 Camelwood
Ellsville, MO 63021
314-227-6440

142

Thad Ferrell on *Cheerio Bowl,* Jackson Falls

The best route is
Think of the most exposed, remote, high-altitude
The North Face.
locations on earth and then think of The North Face.

Photo by Chris Noble

The North Face products offer the most advanced ice, rock, and all-terrain climbing clothing and gear available. Made to weather extremes, The North Face has been the choice of the world's finest mountaineers, polar explorers and skiers for nearly 30 years.

See our new store at **John Hancock Center** 875 N. Michigan Avenue 312•337•7200.
Stores also located in **Oakbrook Center** 708•990•0303   **Woodfield Shopping Center** 708•240•1725

The North Face Store. Explore it.

144

Michael Simpson on *Voice*, Jackson Falls

David Groth on *Zen Arcade*, Jackson Falls

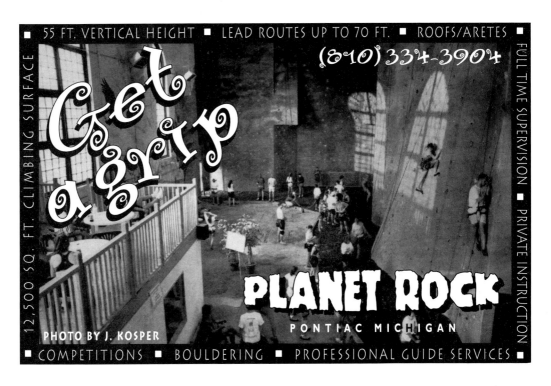

145

Andy Boone bouldering at Devil's Standtable, Giant City

Michael Simpson bouldering above the brim, Spleef Peak, Jackson Falls

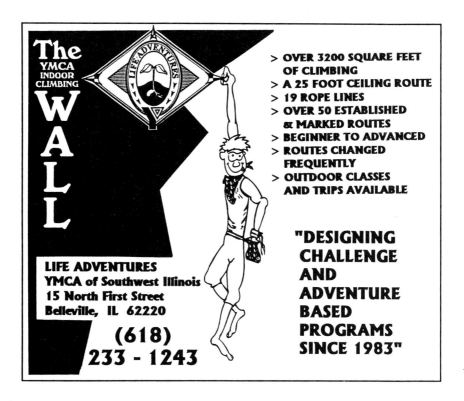

Cedar Bluff stone

Boat required for this bouldering area

Second West

This book is our ad.

Call About Limited Edition Guidebooks　　**618-549-1189**

Hardbound Collectors Edition • Spiral Edition

P.O. Box 3873 Carbondale Illinois 62902

John Sommerhof on *1,2,3*, Giant City

Russell Rowlands on *Group Therapy*, Jackson Falls

Kathy Ulner on *Birthday Route,* Jackson Falls

Kathy Hope on *Return to Forever* traverse, Shelter One Bluff, Giant City

AMBULANCE DIRECTORY

IF YOU'RE AT: **CALL:**

Giant City State Park------------------------------ Jackson County Ambulance
                                                    684-5678 from the Lodge
                                                    911 from Makanda
Fountain Bluff-------------------------------------- **911**

Draper's Bluff-------------------------------------- Johnson County Ambulance
                                                    658-2131
Cedar Bluff--- **658-2131**
Ferne Clyffe State Park---------------------------- **658-2131**

Jackson Falls--------------------------------------- Johnson County Ambulance
                                                    658-2131, or
                                                    Pope County Ambulance
                                                    683-5005

Devil's Kitchen Lake------------------------------- Lifeline Ambulance
                                                    993-3019, or
                                                    Williamson County
                                                    Ambulance
                                                    993-3350

HOSPITAL DIRECTORY

Lourdes Hospital
1530 Lone Oak Rd.
Paducah, KY
(502) 444-2444

Marion Memorial Hospital
917 W. Main
Marion, IL
(618) 997-5341

Herrin Hospital
201 S. 14th
Herrin, IL
(618) 942-2171

Memorial Hospital of Carbondale
404 W. Main
Carbondale, IL
(618) 549-0721

St. Joseph Memorial Hospital
800 N. 2nd
(Rt. 127 North)
Murphysboro, IL
(618) 684-3156

Jennifer Hart

David Hart (seated) & Eric Ulner waiting for the flash at Shelter One Bluff, Giant City

Eric Ulner has been climbing since 1977. Since 1993, he's been operating the Vertical Heartland Climbing School. David Hart has been a photographer since 1990. He owns Egyptian Photo Lab in Carbondale.

GO ROCK CLIMBING!

Bethany Davidson

David Hart / Second West

The mission of Vertical Heartland Climbing School is to teach rock climbing skills including: climber safety, physical movement and body awareness, technical equipment usage and methods, communication, and respect for the vertical environment. We believe that the experience of rock climbing can foster personal development, accomplishment, camaraderie, confidence, and self-control.

Director, Eric Ulner is a professional member of the American Mountain Guides Association and a licensed Emergency Medical Technician.

Ask us about our Mail-Order Catalog

VERTICAL HEARTLAND
CLIMBING SCHOOL
RESERVATIONS (618) 549-1189

2631 Old US Highway 51, Makanda, Illinois 62958 ■ Reservations are preferred at least 2 weeks in advance. A 50% deposit is required at the time of reservation. Balances are due before beginning a class. ■ Deposits are refundable if cancellation occurs 7 days prior to class. ■ Inclement weather can cause class postponement. Course prices are subject to change.

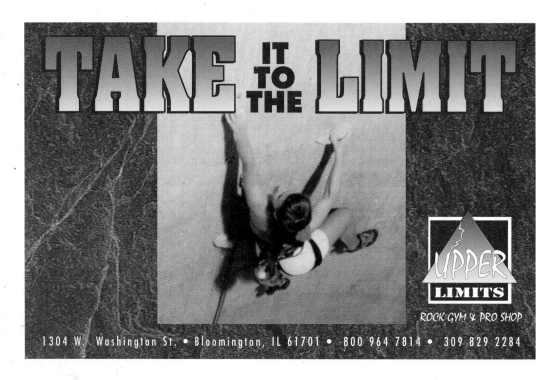

Gary Braaten bouldering at Jackson Falls